JUST LIKE YOU

JUST LIKE YOU

GANGAJI

BY

ROSLYN MOORE

DO

PUBLISHING

The interviews for *Just Like You* were conducted
from August, 2001 to October, 2002.

Cover photographs of Gangaji by Dan Baumbach
Cover and interior book design by Colored Horse Studios

DO Publishing
P.O. Box 103
Mendocino, CA 95460
(707) 964-2630

ISBN 0-9646999-2-3
Library of Congress Catalog Card Number: 2002115639

"THIS IS AN INVITATION to shift your allegiance from the activities of your mind to the eternal presence of your Being."

— Gangaji

PREFACE

*J*ust *Like You* wasn't Gangaji's idea; it was mine. Even though she shares much about herself in her meetings, I have always wanted more. Since we met in 1996, I've paid close attention to her. I see her as living proof of the possibility of fully realizing one's true identity, and I've often found myself trying to piece together her life story. When I heard her say, "The only story worth telling is one that points to the end of the story," I was sure that if she would agree to talk more completely about her life, it would benefit not only me, but many.

This first-hand account is drawn from fourteen interviews that took place at Gangaji's home in northern California. It includes material from her public meetings and from two interviews I did with her for *Meeting Papaji*, a book about her teacher.

After drafting a manuscript from our interviews, Gangaji and I carefully went over the text together. Then I added an opening talk from one of her public meetings, the pictures, and some of the letters she exchanged with Papaji—a special gift. Gangaji was generous with her time and attention, but at every step the initiative was mine.

After our second meeting, as she was standing in her driveway and I was in my car waving good-bye, it occurred to me, "Her life is just an ordinary life. It's not really that different from mine." That's when I realized that when Gangaji says, "As well as *being* you, I am just *like* you," she means it.

Like us, she has a past. She has a house, a car, relationships, a personality, latent tendencies. She has a physical body and the certain knowledge that it was born and it will die. And yet, in her presence, the freedom she points to is alive and apparent. Every meeting we had, every exchange, every note and fax that passed between us was filled with the shining happiness of being she clearly and innocently transmits. Whether she is in New York City having satsang with hundreds of people or at home affectionately scolding her cat, there is the same radiant transparency.

Gangaji's complete candor was intoxicating and our work went along easily, but as it was ending I saw that the manuscript didn't convey her true stature. The question arose, "Why publish an account of Gangaji's life? Isn't there too much of the mundane in it? Won't knowing her story distract people from what she is here to say?"

The answer is no. At least, it needn't be a distraction. This book is here, in part, to free us from the belief that if we know the humanness of a life, we can't attend to the sanctity of that life. Each and every one of us exists where the mundane and the infinite meet. Because Gangaji knows that so well about herself, she helps us know it about ourselves.

Gangaji often says that she wasn't born awake, or under an auspicious star, or to enlightened parents, and that if *she* could wake up, anyone can. For me, it was necessary to write down her story in order to believe this. Once I had, I realized how little her life story really matters. Surely it is fascinating and full of insights, as stories often are. It is even a story of resolution, which is a rare and beautiful thing. But the fulfillment of the spiritual quest is not to be found, or lost, in any story—Gangaji's, or our own. So, the demystification of her story has been very useful to me. And without false glorification, there has been room for even deeper and more genuine love to bloom.

I have a lifelong tendency to probe, to want to know more about someone than meets the eye, but *Just Like You* is the result of a much more serious purpose than curiosity. It is offered as a book of liberation. Whether you think you don't know Gangaji when you pick it up, or you think you do, my fervent wish is that what you imagine to be true is challenged, so that the *unimagined* truth she points to, and transmits, can kiss you.

Roslyn Moore   Mendocino   November, 2002

WELCOME

At her public meetings most of Gangaji's time is spent talking with people one-to-one about what is most important to them. Even so, she often begins by speaking to all who are present. This is a taste of one of her opening talks.

HELLO EVERYONE. WELCOME. Are there people here who have never been in a meeting with me, either in person, or by video or audio?

Let me say, in as few words as I can, why I have appeared in your consciousness at this time in your life. Essentially, it is to offer you the invitation that my teacher gave me, and then sent me to offer to you. The invitation is to stop all of your searching for happiness, for enlightenment, for fulfillment, for being good, for being better, for succeeding, for attaining, for getting. Just stop for one moment. Really, truly stop. Not stop to get, but stop to stop. And in that moment, when your mind activity stops, or even as the mind activity continues, it is possible to recognize what *is* stopped. What is already and always stopped. Then there is the possibility of the full flowering of the realization that who you are is what all of your searching and attaining and getting has been trying to reach.

This is very simple. Often people ask, "If it is so simple, why do so few realize it?" But the answer really is because it is so simple. In the past only the few have been willing to be that simple. Only the few have been willing to truly take the chance of getting nothing, of getting nowhere, of attaining nothing. This possibility can strike fear into the chords of misidentification.

The invitation is simple. The stopping itself is simple. And the realization that is revealed naturally and effortlessly in stopping is endless. Truly endless. Until finally the totality of Being is inclusive as Oneself, beyond any concept of either complex or simple.

It turns out that what we have been avoiding in all of our seeking, and frantically practicing, and frantically gaining and then losing, and then gaining again and then losing again, is the totality of Being. We have been seeking to only have the good parts and to keep out the bad parts, at all costs. But the cost has been the liberation of oneself as the **totality** of Being.

We have all been deeply programmed in one way or another, either in this lifetime or in the genetic structure of the human being, to believe that at the core of who we are there is darkness, there is badness, there is sin. Along with that conditioning comes the belief that we have to spend our time fixing that core, getting away from that core, or creating a better being. In the avoidance of what we suspect we are, however gross or subtle that avoidance may be, we sell our souls to some image of purity or goodness or enlightenment. This activity has been going on for a long, long time.

But if you have sold your soul to some image of who you think you should be, you know it. However good you get at it, finally, you know you are faking it.

The willingness to disrobe to yourself, to be naked to yourself, is the essence of this invitation; to really see yourself all the way, without recourse to any props of any religion, any philosophy, any belief. Not Advaita Vedanta. Not Buddhism. Not Christianity. Not Sufism. Not Judaism. Not New-Ageism, Paganism, or Goddessism. Not anything. The willingness is to be naked with no prop, no belief, nothing that will help you get to the other shore. For an instant, you have to be willing to see yourself as you are.

Then self-inquiry, which is Ramana's gift, is natural and real. Then inquiry is not a mental exercise that is used as another prop to get you out of what you think it is you have to escape. Self-inquiry pulls you back into that which you imagine to be somebody, or some darkness, or some incompleteness, or some unenlightenment, so that you can really and fully ask the question, *who* is suffering, *who* is searching, *who* is unenlightened?

When you ask this question with no agenda and with the willingness to really see, you see that who you thought or think you are does not exist. It is an image. When you are willing to see the non-existence of who you think yourself to be, then it is quite natural, quite effortless, for the truth of who you are to reveal itself. That truth is not another image. It is not the super-human image that you were trying to get to so you could get away from the so-called "little self."

I am not saying there is "bigger self." There is only one Self, and it is not an object. It is the universal subject with no form, yet inhabiting every form.

❖ ❖ ❖ ❖ ❖

I was trying to say that in as few words as possible, but I got carried away. I'll attempt to say it more directly.

You are not who you think you are, however horrible or great that may be. *You are not who you think you are.* To give up the search, to stop, is to recognize that whoever you think you are, and the continued following of that thought, is an avoidance of the truth of who you are.

Our time together is an opportunity to realize that. And if there is no immediate realization, to bring up questions and reports so that we can explore them. Then we can see what the reality is of whatever blocks immediate realization. Then this time, this precious time, this precious lifetime, this moment in time, is not tossed away.

This whole lifetime will be over very soon, but it need not have been in vain. I take our meeting very seriously. I honor it in my heart. I welcome your questions and reports, and I welcome *you.*

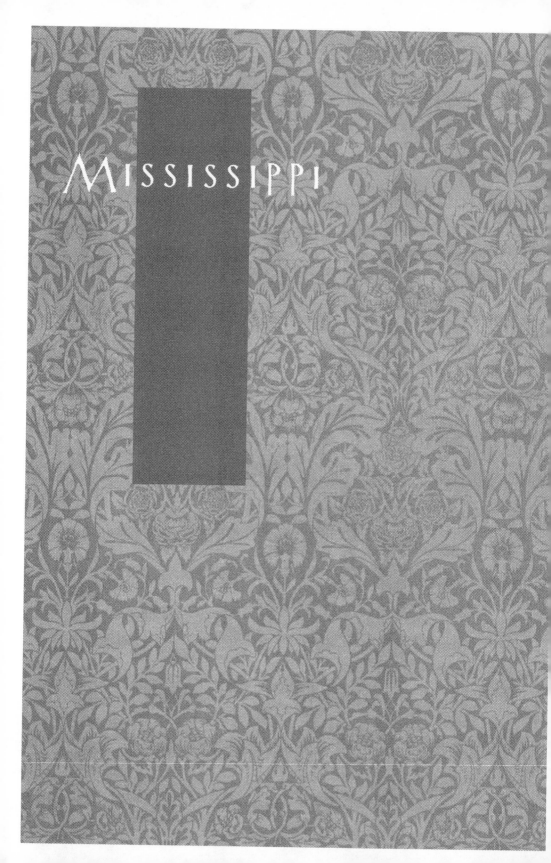

MISSISSIPPI

WHEN I WAS BORN IN 1942 my parents named me Merle Antionette Roberson, but I was always called Toni. At the time my mother got pregnant with me my father was working for the FBI in New York. As a true southerner, he didn't want any child of his to have "New York" on her birth certificate. He contacted another southerner, J. Edgar Hoover, the head of the FBI, and arranged to get himself transferred to Texas just so I could

be born in the South. When I was still a baby my parents moved back to Mississippi where they were from and settled in my father's hometown.

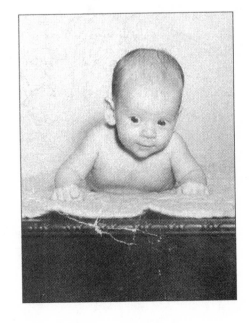

Clarksdale, Mississippi, where I grew up, is actually famous for being the home of the Blues, but most of us white people didn't know anything about that. Once it was the center of an affluent, cotton-growing culture, and when I was a child it still had some of the pretentiousness of that era. The population then was about twenty thousand—ten thousand white and ten thousand black.

In so many ways my childhood was absolutely fine. Clarksdale was a safe place where kids could run around freely. My family lived in a quasi-colonial house in an old neighborhood with lots of big trees. I had an older brother and eventually I had a younger sister. My mother was self-involved which allowed us plenty of space. I always felt that my brother was there to take care of me. Once, years later, he apologized for how he had treated me, but I don't remember him treating me badly. I loved my little sister even though she did drive me crazy at times.

Do you know the book *To Kill A Mockingbird*? It's told from the point of view of a young girl growing up in a southern town that was a lot like my own. And my father was a small-town lawyer too, like Atticus Finch, the girl's father in the story. I was a tomboy and went barefoot and just sort of ran wild. All summer I played kick-the-can with the neighborhood kids. There was a kind of freedom in that life that was really quite wonderful. I loved it.

But when I look back in another way I can see what a mess my childhood was. There was no strong, benevolent parent like Atticus Finch. I remember looking at my family when I was little, looking at my mother and father, and thinking, "There has been a big mistake."

I see myself sitting on the curb in front of our house. I'm maybe eight years old. It is probably summertime, hot and humid, and my family is in distress. My mother is drunk inside and I'm saying to myself, "Something's really wrong here. This is not the family I am supposed to have. This is not the way it is supposed to be." And I began looking for escape, for a way out of an impossible setup.

My father's family was furious when he married my mother. The two of them had met at Ole Miss, the University of Mississippi. As a kid I had the impression it was an idyllic meeting. He was a football player. She was a cheerleader. He was from a good Mississippi family and starting out as a young lawyer when they eloped. Even though her family probably had as much money as his, it wasn't a "good" family. Money alone wasn't how people's social position was judged in the South. Lineage meant more, and my father's lineage was good.

Not only did my mother not have the lineage, she was clearly wild and rebellious. She didn't fit in with the society she married into. She wasn't one of them, so she saw through the falseness and absurdity of their lives as only an outsider could. I remember how she would roll her eyes and declare, "Clarksdale society!" in her disparaging tone of voice. She was never fully embraced by my father's family and their peers.

She was a strong, bright woman and she liked to get drunk. It was her release. When I was growing up I felt oppressed by my mother's wildness. Of course, as a child, I didn't have the maturity to put myself in her shoes and see what she was going through. She was an alcoholic, so

3

her wildness, though it may have started as free-spirited-
ness, became a bondage for her. For me, being her child
was hard.

4

Only one thing interested my mother and that was
having a good time. Fun was her M.O. When she was in
college in the thirties that's what her set did, and she tried
to keep right on doing it. Of course, that's not possible—
not the way she liked to do it. Physiologically, she was a
true alcoholic.

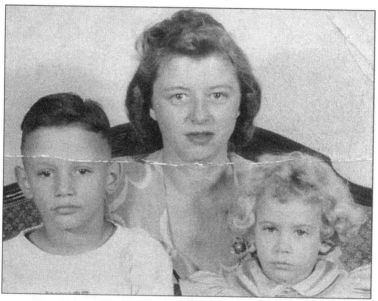

MY BROTHER, MOTHER AND ME

She was only interested in herself. She certainly didn't
have much interest in being a good mother, so my
brother, sister and I were always competing for whatever
scraps of her attention we could get. That kept us isolated
from each other.

On the upside, she was very smart and funny, and we had some good times. She was good at telling jokes and my friends loved her. When they came over we would sit around the kitchen table and visit with my parents. Even as youngsters we did that. There were times when my mother would maybe be a little high on alcohol and she'd be so entertaining, so much fun. She had the kind of southern style where she could lift people up with her quick wit and easy humor.

I was in love with her. I absolutely was in love with my mother. But it was a frustrating love affair because she was so *bad*. Along with her ability to lift you up, she had the ability to make you feel really horrible. She was completely unreliable.

I was in love with her, and I was ashamed of her. I didn't want her to be the way she was. She saw that, and it

made her angry. She wasn't going to change. She was a tough woman on the outside. I was too sensitive for her. She would say to me, "Stop putting on," a southern phrase for, "Stop putting on such a show." I was always too "too" for her: too sensitive, too dramatic, too over-the-top. She was over-the-top herself, but in her own way.

For instance, she cursed. Women in the South in the fifties didn't curse, but she did. You wouldn't believe the words that came out of her mouth! I was humiliated, and so was my father's family. That's a little bit of how the family dynamic worked.

I desperately wanted her to change. When I was eight or nine I started writing her letters asking her not to drink any more and telling her how much it hurt me. I would leave them on the nightstand next to her bed, imagining her waking up and reading them. But if she did, I never knew about it. She never said a word about any of them. The message was clear: Don't bother me. Don't bring me down.

People almost never got divorced in that generation, and my father just went along with my mother. She was his wife. But I know he was angry. He had horrible migraines and heart trouble, among other ailments. My parents fought often, but I think they had a very passionate marriage for, say, the first twenty years.

My father drank with my mother and he drank a lot, but he wasn't a true alcoholic like she was. Later, after my mother died and he'd remarried, he and his wife would have an evening cocktail or an occasional glass of wine, but that was all. Drinking wasn't a disease for him. For my mother, it was a real poison to her system.

Not that my father was a great drunk, and not that I wanted to be around him when he'd been drinking. He'd get slurry-speech drunk, but he wasn't a fall-down-pass-out drunk like my mother. He went to sleep in bed, in his pajamas. I minded his drinking, but not like I minded my mother's.

I always felt that my father loved me. I was always secure in that, even though he rarely showed it. Neither parent ever said "I love you" that I can remember. But I have a memory of sitting on my father's lap when I was five while he brushed my hair. We had a sweet relationship.

My father wanted me to be a certain way—pretty and a good student—and to make him proud. That's the way I wanted to be too. I prayed to Jesus to be those things. A big thrust of my life was toward conformity and respectability. Early on I formulated what the perfect mother would be like, what the perfect life would be like. It would definitely be respectable.

Of her three children my mother liked me the least. I don't think she was always a bad parent. My earliest years were probably okay, and I'm pretty sure she was affectionate when I was a baby. I know I was breast-fed. She was young then so the alcoholism wasn't entrenched.

She was a strange creature though. She loved her babies, but as we grew older she didn't like us so much. "I love babies. I don't like children, but I love babies." She said this often, and I believe it was true. She was a very sensual woman. Maybe she wasn't comfortable with her sensuality around children. I don't know.

8

My first memory is of being about four years old, going to Florida with my mother's parents, losing my shoes and feeling that it was all okay. In this particular memory, in the roundness and fullness of it, I have that sense: I'm okay. So I guess my first few years weren't bad. But when I was six my mother had a new little baby. My sister.

That was my first year of misery.

chapter two

AFTER MY SISTER was born I began having intense experiences of losing my body. It would get small, very small, and thin like the edge of a paper, and then my body was gone.

The first time it happened was when I was napping in my parents' bed. I had a fever and woke up from a nightmare. Everybody else was downstairs. I was terrified. When I ran to my mother she was nonchalant. Later, as the experience kept recurring, she became concerned.

I couldn't keep my body here. It would become non-existent, made up of nothing at all. Maybe doctors have a name for it, when the body appears to disappear. It was a horrible loss of control for me. My mother was adoring her new baby, and I felt as if I'd lost her. That may be why I started having these experiences. Maybe they were anxiety attacks. That could have been it—a six-year-old's anxiety attack.

My mother took me to Memphis to a psychiatrist who gave me a lot of ink-blots to look at. He didn't talk to me or comfort me or anything like that. He wasn't that kind of psychiatrist.

He gave me pills. Phenobarbitol, eighth-of-a-grain

tablets. He told me to take one whenever the experience started to happen. After that, when the feeling came, that horrible feeling that my body was starting to go, I took one of those little pills, swallowed it, and Whoa! Body back, chair back, mind could rest.

Except that it couldn't really rest. Something wanted out. Something painful and unacceptable was being sent back to the dungeon.

Later I heard that the psychiatrist told my mother that she should be touching me more, but I don't remember that she ever did. At that time we had a black maid named Suzie who had a really big bosom. When I started to feel my body disappear, before they gave me the pills, I'd run to her and lay my little head in the curve of her breast, and oh boy! That was great. That was safety. My body didn't come back, but it didn't matter. There was love there.

I took those phenobarbitols until I was nineteen. Amazing. All those years. If I got overly anxious or couldn't sleep, I'd take one, and I appreciated having them. They helped me get by. But I finally put them aside. I'm not sure why I was able to stop, but I just knew it was time. I was at college by then, away from home and the misery of my relationship with my mother. I knew I was strong enough to do without them.

Polio and tuberculosis were spreading through the South in the late forties, and everybody was afraid. There was a place called a preventorium, an institution in a camp-like setting where parents sent their kids to beef them up so they wouldn't get sick. People were coming out of the Depression and they wanted their children plump and healthy. I was a real skinny kid and I got sick a lot. The same year I began taking the pills my parents sent me to the preventorium. It was in Jackson, Mississippi, about a four hour drive from Clarksdale.

When it comes to health there have always been two themes in my life, running side by side. One is strong and tomboyish, athletic and energetic. The other is an acute physical hypersensitivity, along with an emotional hypersensitivity. The physical and the emotional feed on each other. When I'm strong, I'm really strong, but my body can go off very quickly and then I'm sick. It was like that when I was a kid. My skinniness was a big deal then, and it was often talked about. My parents told me, "Drink your milk or we're going to send you to the preventorium."

But I hated milk. I couldn't drink it. And they sent me away.

I was furious! It was like I was being punished for not drinking my milk, and then when I got to the preventorium they still made me drink it there. I felt totally abandoned. The place didn't have a good feeling, nothing like summer camp, which I loved. I'm sure my parents believed they were doing the right thing. It cost them some money to send me, and it was something that lots of families were doing, but I hated it.

My biggest fear was that I would be left there in the summer. They made you wear these little outfits, bloomers and tops, but I heard that in the summers the little girls didn't wear tops. Even though I was only six years old I was petrified. I mean, a girl should wear a top!

In a picture taken when my family came to visit me at the preventorium, one I can't find, the new baby is in my mother's arms, with my brother and father standing close to them, beaming with happiness. My parents are in their thirties and they're looking good—this shining family—and then there's me standing slightly to the side with my arms crossed. I'm scowling. I'm wearing these funny-looking bloomers and a sweater that's buttoned askew. I am mad and definitely showing it.

One night I lay awake in my bed in the preventorium after the other kids had fallen asleep. It was a large room full of iron beds, like big baby cribs. I was so unhappy, so lonesome, so sad. There was a true homesickness, a really deep kind of wailing. That's when I realized, "I'm miserable here. I am an unhappy person." It was the first time I remember the thought forming that I was unhappy—that

I was unworthy and a castoff—and it was the beginning of my identification of myself as a sufferer.

Just then, right when I was having those thoughts, I had the strong sense of something watching over me, protecting me. I felt a living presence in the room. In Sunday school we'd been taught that we had guardian angels. In that dark, uninviting dormitory, feeling as miserable as I ever had, I sensed what I took to be an angel watching over me—large and beautiful and alive. I was still lonely and sad, but I wasn't alone. That's a memory that's locked in.

When I went back to school, back home, I was enrolled in the neighborhood Catholic school because it could get me up to speed academically. That way when I entered public school the following year I wouldn't have to lose a grade. So I went from the preventorium right into Catholic school.

It was a horrible school. We were taught by old-timey nuns in long black habits with white wimples and heavy metal crosses. And they were mean nuns, or at least they were mean to me. I was not a Catholic, and I was often late because my mother wouldn't get up out of bed early enough to fix my breakfast so I could get to school on time. So there was this humiliation: I was late coming into the school year, I was late in the morning, and I was punished.

My parents knew I was going to go to the public school the next year, and they wanted me to join the Brownie Scouts there. The Catholic school also had the Brownie Scouts and I was asked to join them too. Not knowing what else to do, I said yes to both groups. They met on the same day, which meant that I had to miss every other time. Both of the troop leaders were angry with me, asking, "Why are you absent so much?" and I would lie about where I was. My mother didn't even know I was in two troops because she wasn't paying enough attention to me to know. The crux of it came on the day of the scout parade.

All the troops are going to be in the big parade, but I am in two troops. I have on my little Brownie uniform, and I march through the town for a while with the Catholic school group, then I run up and march for a while with the public school group, this seven-year-old doing the Brownie Scout thing.

That was the way my life felt, just kind of running— running to catch up and to fit in somewhere. And I wasn't fitting in with either group because I wasn't really *there* with either of them. Now I can laugh at it, but it was a mess. It was a real mess.

In the midst of the confusion and anguish of that year, I fell in love with Christ, blissfully and surrenderingly in love. There were benevolent pictures of Christ and statues of Mary everywhere at the school. They made a strong impression on me. Even though a few of us were not Catholics—there was a Jewish kid, and I was an Episcopalian, and there was a Chinese girl—we still had to sit in on the catechism.

I had gone to Sunday school, but this was totally different. The nuns weren't just telling us Bible stories. They were really trying to put the fear of God and the love and redemption of Christ into us, and a religious fire was awakened in me.

Catechism classes were every day before the school lessons started. I was absorbing the teachings. I started believing what was taught and took the lessons into my heart. I did feel a little bad because I was maybe going to burn in hell, since I wasn't a Catholic. That's what they told us. But overriding that, I felt the love of Christ and its promise. I got that there is this Savior, that there is love and it is available to me. I discovered a warmth, a place of refuge and rest.

I fell deeply in love with Mary too, who was a devoted mother. That's when I began praying. I prayed to Jesus, to Mary and to my guardian angel. When I began displaying my unrestrained love for Jesus, talking about it, and overflowing with it, my parents didn't like it. They felt threatened.

I started building little shrines for Mary all over our house. My parents were dismayed and took them down. They didn't believe in that. It was too much for them, too over the top. We were Christian, but the message that came through was, "Let's not take this too far. We don't want to go to extremes here." So I began to try to control this huge love because it was unacceptable.

I perceived that the hugeness of love, the uncontrollableness of it, is not safe. It is not what my parents, who were my gods, wanted. They wanted me to keep it in. Since I was basically an insecure child hoping to find security and love from my parents, I stuffed it. I tried to model what it was my parents wanted me to be: a success-ful child who would become a successful woman who would breed successful children—and then die!

In retrospect, I see that out of that repression a search developed. Love went unconfirmed and got fixated exter-nally. For me, as happens so often, first it was fixated on my mother, but my experience was, "She's unreliable and I will be discarded when something fresh comes along." Then Jesus appeared. When I saw him, it was, "Oh, here is the loving face that loves little children." We used to sing a song in church that I really believed: "Jesus loves me, this I know, for the Bible tells me so." Jesus took the place of my mother as my love object. But that also didn't work. So the search became established. Even decades later, when I was looking for the Buddha or enlightenment, it was an expression of that same search for an external love object.

By this time I was already in the public school, and I became a little Protestant girl. The heart opening that had happened went dormant. It was covered, and in the cov-ering of it I was miserable again, but not as miserable as before. And I was praying. I prayed throughout my child-hood. I prayed for things—to be popular, for a new dress, for forgiveness, to be a good girl, for my mother to stop drinking—because that's how I knew to pray. But I knew I loved Jesus, and I knew Jesus loved me. I see that reli-gion serves when you are not getting that love from your family and it is offered by a teaching, a teacher, or a savior.

There was a sweet little Episcopal church around the corner from our house. My parents used to go to that

church, but that ended once the drinking really came in.
I was sent to Sunday school and confirmed there when I
was twelve. I continued to go there sporadically after my
confirmation, and then that stopped.

All my young life I avoided fully surrendering to the
love of Christ I felt because of the fear of where it would
lead me. When I was eight or nine I went to a couple of
Baptist revival meetings with a neighborhood friend.
These big evangelical tent meetings would come to our
town. We Episcopalians thought they were just so tacky.
It was like, "What are they doing? Where is their
restraint?"

But attending those meetings I felt a deep fire burning inside. I sensed if I actually surrendered to the fire I
would turn into some kind of a traveling, evangelical
preacher lady. Since I wanted to be acceptable to my parents, that was my great fear. Instead, I looked for
satisfaction in other experiences, and the call to confirm
God, to speak out, to shout "Hallelujah! Amen!" was
denied. It made me laugh when, after the first satsang I
ever held, someone approached me and said, "Thank you
for preaching the Gospel."

chapter three

As I got older my mother's drinking got worse. Earlier on she would get drunk every day, and then she would stop for a while. "Going on the wagon" is what they would call it. But later she didn't even try to stop, and then her drinking would start in the morning. The worst times were Christmas, or whenever there was a big holiday. That gave her an excuse to start drinking really early. Right after breakfast there would be champagne cocktails. By noon she'd be drunk. That's when she got sloppy, and I'd respond to it viscerally—like there was a hot knife slicing through me.

When I was nine or ten a couple of us were playing at a friend's house, and our mothers were spending the time together. I think that the woman whose house it was must have been an alcoholic too. The mothers started drinking while the kids played. My mother got very drunk.

That alone was painful. Then I had to call my father at his law office to tell him my mother was drunk and couldn't drive us home. He came and got us, and he was mad at my mother. She wouldn't speak to me for a week because I had told on her.

Oh my God, that was agonizing. And she was furious! I just hadn't known what to do. I saw her falling-down-drunk in front of my friends, which was already horrible. Then, that she wouldn't speak to me was devastating. She was punishing me by ignoring me, by not speaking to me or looking at me.

It got to the point that whenever my friends came to my house my mother did something that embarrassed me. I remember a friend saying, "*My* mother would never do that!" I stopped having people come over. It was just too dangerous. I couldn't control it. I think that's the thing about being a child of alcoholic parents. It gets to where you're always trying to control the damage, and it's exhausting. Besides the pain and anguish of the disease, there's a child trying to control what can't be controlled.

I have to mention my grandmother, my mother's mother. We called her Mammy. She lived with us at different times, not for long periods, but she was a great source of love. She really saved my life—she and a couple of the servants that we had. Mammy loved me unconditionally. She always told me I was the greatest person in the world. She told my brother and sister that too. She fixed our hair and played with us and truly enjoyed being with us. She loved to hold me and take care of me, and she always communicated her pleasure in me. I would sleep with her when she came to visit. She teased that I made her deaf by knocking her on the head with a porcelain doll I demanded the right to sleep with. I really don't know what my life would have been like without her.

MAMMY, YEARS LATER

My mother was always a narcissist, and as I became a teenager she began to be jealous of me. I can see that now, but I didn't see it then. I was this blossoming young woman in the house. She called me "Camille," who was a consumptive, dying heroine in a French play. She was right—I was overly dramatic—but she had a kind of biting sarcasm that was just plain mean, especially when she'd been drinking. There were spells of her treating me kindly, like I remember her getting out her sewing machine and making me a dress, but mostly she would criticize me and put me down. Of course, she would certainly tell this story differently!

When I began dating I had to make sure my date picked me up by a certain time and brought me back after a certain time because there was this block of time when, if my date came into the house, he'd see my mother drunk. Then, when I got home afterwards, she'd be passed out on the floor of the landing going up the stairs. It was extremely difficult for me because I took it so personally.

Talking to my brother and sister about our childhood, it doesn't seem that my mother's alcoholism got to them the way it got to me. For one thing, my mother and sister had a good relationship. They were buddies. My brother had a rougher time with our mother, but neither my brother nor my sister is high-strung like I am. They are more solid. Of course, part of being hypersensitive is thinking you are suffering more than anyone else. When I step back and look at it I don't know for sure I was having the hardest time.

Until I was a teenager, during the nights when I was too agitated to fall asleep, I would get into my sister's bed so we could sleep together. I was always aware that her physical energy was very different from mine. She was six years younger, but she was so much more grounded than I was that being next to her would calm me. I was the older sister, mean and bossy and all of that, but in that one way I would take refuge in her settledness.

I mentioned the picture of me scowling with my family at the preventorium. Actually, if you were to look at our family pictures, you'd see that I look angry and miserable in almost every one of them until I'm twelve or thirteen. That's when I began to smile, and I smiled a lot.

When I was in the seventh grade there was a dance that I didn't get invited to. At the time I thought, "Wait a minute. I've *got* to be liked, I *have* to be popular. I have to *do* something." Cold-bloodedly, I planned out what to do. I'd read an article in a magazine that told you how to be popular. It was simply a matter of saying hello to everyone you saw, calling them by their names, and smiling at them. I went after it.

Even though it was fake at first, it was one of those things that fed on itself. The friendlier I was the more I was liked, and the more I was liked the friendlier I felt. In high school I was very popular and had a lot of friends, three really close ones. That was wonderful because, with the shift of attention onto my social life, I began to be less dependent on the family dynamic for my identity. I became a cheerleader and was the homecoming queen of my school.

Queen Toni, Homecoming Court to Reign At Clarksdale-Jackson Central Combat

Toni Roberson (left) will reign as Homecoming Queen tonight. Lady Margaret Fyfe will be Maid of Honor.

But on another level I could say that, even then, my time was spent running from despair. In my search for a love object I was attempting to make myself attractive so my love could fixate on my own mirrored image. Making myself into someone who was popular was a strategy of escape. Later, when I made a good marriage, it was the same thing. When I became a mother—same again. And when I became a spiritual seeker, it was the same. Underneath all those experiences was a desperation to escape the void, empty of hope and life and spirit, that I secretly feared was my true face.

I never met the standard for pretty in the South. There was a specific look, which was round—big breasts, tiny waist, round face, round bottom—and I was not that type. If there's a beauty here it's from something else, and I didn't know about it then because nobody was interested in it. My mother told me I wasn't pretty and that I really needed to develop my personality. She said that a lot. Only my grandmother thought I was pretty—beautiful, she said—and that was marvelous. That was her love eyes.

For a southern girl prettiness was supreme because that's what was supposed to get her the best husband. The ideal was to be pretty and for boys to be falling in love with you. I had only two boyfriends in all of high school, which made me feel like a failure as a southern belle. If I'd succeeded I would have probably never left the South, so it was a great failure. I bow down before that failure.

I'd always been a good student, but by the time I got out of high school I'd fallen in love with learning. Until then I was a nervous student, mostly because I hated tests. I was one of those people who would study very hard for a test until I knew the material backwards and forwards, then go into the test sweating and tense, expecting to fail. One evening, studying in my room, I had a flash that I

loved what I was doing. It was thrilling, and the very possibility that I *could* fail was what gave it life.

After that I fully enjoyed my studies. I loved English,
literature and Spanish. I wasn't good in math so I can't say
I loved that, but doing homework was no longer a chore.
I looked forward to it. The joy of learning just grew and
grew and grew. That was a great gift. That *is* a great gift.

chapter four

THERE WAS NEVER any question about whether or not I would go to college, and there was never any question as to which college it would be. It was always Ole Miss. My parents were dedicated alumni, and going there was part of being loyal to Mississippi and the South. It was fine with me. At first my father wanted me to study to be a secretary, but he gave way and I was able to study liberal arts. I was happy to go to college. I loved it, and I joined a sorority.

At Ole Miss something happened that caused a major change in my life's direction. For some reason teachers from the Ivy League universities started taking sabbaticals so they could teach in southern schools for a year or two. This was in the early sixties, right before the whole integration of the South and the rioting. I had a history teacher and a philosophy teacher, one from Harvard and one from Yale.

In my freshman year, after one of my philosophy classes, my teacher sat me down and said to me, "You write really good papers, and you are obviously intelligent. I say a lot of questionable things in this class. Why don't you challenge me?" At first I didn't even know what he was talking about. I just drew a blank. Years later, when I was having a meeting in Nashville, part of my frustration was the passivity in the people. What those teachers finally did was cut through a certain kind of conditioned passivity to awaken my natural, inquiring intelligence.

That same year my history teacher blew my mind wide open. He introduced me to a world that was not at all the world I had known. Until then I had never questioned my southern programming. So although I had loved black people in my life, been attended to by them, and had even received the love from them that I hadn't got from my family, I didn't believe they were altogether human. I know it's hard to believe, but that's what being a member of the southern cult did. When I was growing up we were still fighting the Civil War and hoping the South had won, and we hated Abraham Lincoln. We all still wished we had slaves!

In that history class, and another one I took, my mind opened to a much larger perspective. I quickly recognized the horror of what I'd been taught, and felt a burning shame for myself, my family, and my ancestors. All of it.

In the blowing open of the lie I experienced an infusion of love and new life. I knew the life that had been charted for me as a southern woman had been thrown off course in a really big way.

When I went home and shared with my parents how thrilled I was about what I was learning, my father was in absolute shock. Here he had sent me to the only safe school in the country and the "communists" had gotten to me there!

That began a period of schism in my family. A few years later I marched for civil rights with the black and white teachers I taught with. Then I marched against the Vietnam War, so we were in conflict and argued over race relations and politics for years. Still, during those same years, I remember lots of times when I, or a friend and I, sat around the table at my parents' house and we'd drink and visit and laugh.

I became good friends with a girl from Florida who was different from my high school girlfriends. We took that history class together. She was earthy and funny and a lot better educated than I was. She brought more to the table than I was used to and that pushed me. We could talk about life very honestly, something I didn't do with my other friends. She and I hooked up with some people who wouldn't have been unusual in New York but were considered Bohemian in Mississippi.

It was the beginning of a different life for me, an intellectual life. I started to identify myself with the intellectual fringe. I remember going to a football game with three friends after Ole Miss was integrated. Two of the black students were in seats with nobody sitting around them. There were no other seats so we sat down next to them. Although we were liberal leaning, we weren't really trying to make a statement. All four of us had been brought up in the same way, conditioned in the same way, and we were in the process of breaking free of that. My cousin was standing down at the end of the bleachers cursing me and yelling up at me, "Ask them about the Congo! Ask them about the Congo!" It took me a long time to forgive him for that.

In my sophomore year I met the man I was going to marry. His fraternity and my sorority were friendly. We were on the same train going down to New Orleans for a football game. The first time I saw him he was in a group playing cards. When we met I liked him right away. He wasn't part of my new crowd, but before long we started dating. We had an interesting friendship. He was brilliant, quite intellectual, and also an artist.

We had wonderful discussions, and there was passion

ANOTHER POPULAR engaged couple, Toni Roberson and Ferrell Varner Jr., will be entertained tonight at a plantation party in Mississippi. Giving the supper will be Letitia Parchman, Merriwether and John Fargason III and the Duff Holcombs, at Clover Hill, the Fargason home near Clarksdale.

there, youthful passion. Before I met him I had two relationships in college. Both guys were real jerks, and my heart was broken both times. I could see he was a person who would never break my heart, and that was beautiful. I went toward that and I loved him, truly loved him, but in the long run he was too nice. He wasn't wild enough for me. The decision to marry him—that this is what it takes to be happy—came from my mind, and that is probably why it couldn't work. But when I was twenty-three we married.

By then I had finished a year of graduate school in English Literature, and he was going to medical school. We were planning a huge wedding. He was from a "good" southern family. When I considered what it would be like, I thought, "I can't do a big wedding like this. It'll be too humiliating. All these 'respectable' families from Memphis will be coming here, and my mother will be drunk." So I got up my nerve and asked my mother not to drink for the wedding, and she didn't drink until after we left. Then she got really plastered, but she stayed sober while we were there, which was a gift. Maybe she started getting a little more respect for me once I stopped needing her so much.

My relationship with my mother wasn't resolved until she was on her deathbed, but after I left home, married, and was my own woman it improved. In 1967 I had just had Sarah, my daughter. I was visiting my parents and spending time with my girlfriends. My mother and I got into a really big fight—I don't remember what it was about—and she kicked me out. I remember her saying, "You've always looked down your nose at your sister and me." It was true. I had. She demanded I leave the house. I left and got on a plane, and that broke something. I was very emotional about it, but I had a good husband and family to go to. I realized she was no longer my primary reference point. That began some essential unwinding.

The day I got married I already knew the marriage wouldn't survive. That very day, at some level, I knew what would happen. I was using him as a way to escape my family and get out of Mississippi. I didn't know what other options I had. I'd been brought up that you marry well, that's what you do as a woman. And I married well. He was a doctor and a real gentleman, but from the start our marriage was doomed.

chapter five

I LIKED BEING a young wife, though, and that initial knowledge quickly faded. My husband was finishing medical school, we were living in Memphis, and I was teaching school. We were having a good time. I had done what I thought I needed to do to be a success and was riding on it.

We planned for me to get pregnant and I did. I was very happy about it. For the first time I started to become body-conscious. I had never thought much about my body, but when I was pregnant I enjoyed being consciously in touch with my body. Having a baby was fine, and then, Lord, the baby was a shock. Well, maybe the birth was the first shock of the matter.

I was twenty-five then, but I was a really young twenty-five. When it came time to have the baby and I had labor pains I felt like, "What? This is really big. It is *huge*, and it is impossible." I had no idea it would feel like it did, not a clue. I can remember actually having the thought, "This is a big mistake! Wait a minute, I want to get out of this!" But with the stupidity there was some intelligence that said, "You can't get out of it. It's too late. You made the mistake nine months ago." So there was a surrender. In those days, in the South, just about everyone took drugs to kill the pain, but before the drugs kicked in there was a moment of recognition: "Okay, it's here. I'll meet it."

Then I had a baby. Nothing brings you down to earth more than a baby—having to care for the baby. Being a mother was a big surprise, and I was not good at it. You know how some people are just naturally good mothers? I wasn't one of them. Plus, I didn't have good training.

I had been picturing a little one-dimensional, story-book child. I was completely unprepared for a very independent, strong child who actually had desires of her own. After awhile I went back to teaching as a substitute

SARAH AT THREE

teacher. I found good help, a wonderful woman who came every day to take care of Sarah, so things didn't seem to be going badly.

In the summer of 1969 I was teaching school in Memphis and Sarah was two years old. My husband was doing his internship to become a doctor. The picture with which I had entered my marriage was wearing a little thin and I was beginning to tell the truth about my life, at least internally. I was saying, "Yikes! What have I done?" I was seeing that my marriage wasn't the escape I had thought it would be. It didn't deliver the make-believe life I had expected.

I was teaching in a school that was integrated for the first time that year. It happened to be Elvis Presley's old high school. I had forty ninth-graders in my English class, street-wise black kids and poor white kids who hated each other. They'd been taught to be enemies, and they were, so teaching them was tough.

I saw that teaching was real work and to do it you had to be dedicated to it. I had some fun with the kids, and I felt good about what was happening in class, but the work was absolutely exhausting. It became clear that teaching was not my vocation. I was not totally committed to it. It was a play. I was playing at being a teacher, and playing at being a grownup, and playing at being a wife and a mother.

There was a student teacher in my classroom with whom I had an immediate connection. I was young and we didn't have an "I am the teacher, you are the aide" relationship. At the time there was a pretty big split between the people her age and mine. When we met I'd never smoked grass. This was the South. I was drinking alcohol and smoking cigarettes, not smoking grass. She was happy to give me some pot to try.

My husband and I closed the doors and smoked a joint, and it was wonderful. We'd loved drinking, but this was different. We had some music on, some classical music, and I could hear it in a way I had never heard music before. It was a state-of-consciousness change that felt great, so relaxing and different. I wouldn't say the marijuana was exactly a heart opener at that point, but it was an opener. It was a forbidden substance so it was a little scary too. Smoking it meant we were hip and on the edge.

Then Woodstock came along. When I saw the movie I thought, "Oh my God, that's it! That is what I want! 'Getting free' is what will *really* make me happy." It was a different idea of freedom than the one I had grown up with, which had a lot to do with alcohol and partying. Now it was the grass and the hippies and the protesting and the counterculture. It all looked great to me. So I reached for that as a way to get out of this.

When my husband graduated from medical school he was drafted into the army, automatically as a captain, and stationed in the Washington, D.C. area. That was when the real downward spiral started for me. In Memphis I had kept myself very busy and not been so conscious of my dissatisfaction. After we moved I began to admit to myself that I wanted to get out of the confinement of the marriage.

There were things I liked about our new life. We were living in a big apartment complex and had a couple of sets of good friends. We got involved in the anti-war movement, joining in marches against the war, so our activities as a couple were good, but I was less happy with myself. That it was an expansive time showed me how unhappy I really was.

Sarah was a very intense child. She had high energy from the beginning and she was exhausting for me. She didn't sleep through the night until she was five years old. As a doctor in the army my husband wasn't around much, especially because he was doing a lot of moonlighting at night. That was hard. I was doing some substitute teaching, but I had trouble figuring out the day care thing. While I was stagnating in my own house my husband was very happy. I thought if I was miserable then it must be my fault. I would say that's when my neurosis caught up with me.

Sarah and I were spending a lot of time together and I could see I was failing with her. It wasn't that I didn't love her. I felt I loved her, but I was really ignorant and didn't know what was needed. I enjoyed telling her stories and making up endings. We had our moments of pleasure, but I couldn't find the connection, the way in.

Now I see Sarah sensed the lie I was living. She picked up on my internal strife and didn't like it, so we were having a very difficult time. I was immature and impatient. Alone with her at night, I'd scream, "Go to sleep! You are driving me crazy!" Then I would feel bad and go in where she was sleeping, so cute, and stroke her back, whispering, "Your mother loves you, your mother loves you so much."

When my husband's tour in the army was over we were free to leave D.C. He had wonderful artistic talent and I encouraged him to do something with his artwork. I didn't recognize what my own talents were then, which was part of my frustration, but I strongly supported his. From the time I'd seen "Woodstock" I was drawn to the counterculture and wanted to move to California. As a southern woman I was quite accomplished at getting my man to do what I wanted, so when he was accepted by the San Francisco Institute of Art we took the plunge and moved to California.

CALIFORNIA

chapter six

We ARRIVED IN San Francisco. The sun was shining and the air was cool, and I felt completely at home for the first time in my life. I got out of the car in the city and said, "Ah-h! This is *not* Mississippi!"

Once we were in California there was some kind of an explosion in me. I began feeling like I could be more authentically myself. My husband began taking painting classes and working as an emergency room doctor, and I finally told him I wanted a divorce. It was a shock to him—and to everybody—because the marriage looked so good on the outside. I'd really been lying to him, from the bedroom on up.

The situation was incredibly painful. To see him suffering was horrible. I felt totally responsible and full of guilt, and both of our families were angry with me. I was the bad one, because why would I leave him? He was wonderful. That's the truth. He really was. It wasn't as if he was not so wonderful behind closed doors.

But it ended up being a friendly parting and we arranged for joint custody of Sarah. The separation was especially hard for her. She was four years old and had a life going in a certain direction. Then, *blam!*

For Sarah, part of the disaster of our parting was that her father had always been the stable parent. He was the one who'd always held the family together. I went through the motions of it, but he was the depth of it. After I was single I would bring my daughter along with me wherever I went, thinking, "She'll like this too," but

she didn't. What Sarah wanted was her nuclear family back, and it was quite clear I was the one who was responsible for her not having it.

I went to see a therapist. It was right after the separation and I was having kind of a nervous breakdown. There were different types of free clinics around California then. I just walked into an office off the street.

I had seven or eight sessions with a compassionate man, a Freudian psychologist. Simply unburdening myself and speaking honestly about what was happening with me was wonderfully helpful. I had been aware of my emotions but had never really examined and worked with them before. I liked it. That's when I began studying psychology in a layperson's kind of way. I was aware of my unhappiness and it seemed to me that to learn how to be happy would be great. As a teenager I had discovered the pleasure of learning, so why not apply those skills to learning what I wanted to know most? Over the following years I went to different teachers and read a lot. It was all beneficial. I learned what my neurosis was, what my fixation was, what my habits were.

In 1972 the city was overflowing with teachers, and there were no substitute teaching jobs available, so I got a job as a cocktail waitress in a bar on Union Street. It was a jolt. I had never seen myself as a waitress. I found it liberating to let go of an identification of myself as somebody who did a professional thing. Not that there weren't moments of panic. "Oh no, I'm not a teacher? I'm not somebody important and respected? I'm a *cocktail waitress?* Well, yeah, I am a cocktail waitress." I was selling ninety cent beers and going for ten cent tips, and it was really fun. My parents were shocked, but that was part of the fun.

I began to get involved in some other relationships. I was having a great time. I was doing my normal suffering thing—seeking the love, approval, and recognition from friends and lovers that I hadn't received from my mother—but I loved the life I was living. What I loved about it was that it was so unknown and so uncontrollable.

I was making the same mistake I always had, though, by thinking that freedom meant living in a certain way. Before, I'd believed my happiness depended on having certain things—the right husband, the right child, the right social standing. Now I was telling myself that happiness depended on not having those things. I was just exchanging one set of criteria for another.

Luckily, joining the counterculture, smoking grass and then taking psychedelics, helped end my belief that there is any external criterion for happiness. Those substances, if you're really taking them to tell the truth, will show you that all your ideas and beliefs about what happiness depends on are made up. They are all unreliable.

Psychedelics were important in my life, not because I did them a lot—I took maybe five trips—but because the experiences I had on them were so huge. I was introduced to mescaline in Golden Gate Park by a lover who was on a spiritual search, so taking drugs always had a spiritual context for me. I never took them casually.

On that first trip, grace cracked open the very tightly woven story of my life. My story was exposed as nothing in the face of the truth of *life*.

Shortly after taking the mescaline I had the experience of the structures in my mind melting. What had seemed so solid—the way I'd been taught to structure reality—I felt melting in my brain. It was alarming, but my partner was a good guide. He kept telling me to relax, that what was happening to me was okay. In the exact moment I relaxed, I was astonished by the scintillating beauty that was everywhere. I felt like I was seeing what *is* for the first time.

Life as I knew it until then was revealed not to be life as it *is*, and I rededicated my existence to something much bigger than itself. Years later I recognized that what I glimpsed in that experience was the truth of who I am, and looking back now, I see that a line was crossed and that once that line is crossed, everything, even what is most painful, is in service to fully awakening to the Truth.

That's not what it looked like at the time, though. I quickly discounted the reality of the glimpse. When the experience passed I went into a deep misery for having lost the bliss. There was a kind of self-torture. "Where did I misplace it? How do I get it back?" Then came years and years of attempts to find it. Some of the attempts seemed successful, but the next day, or the next moment, the recognition was followed by, "Oh, I've lost it again." The perception came back of my life being in the foreground and this vastness being somewhere in the past and, I hoped, in the future.

When I was a child there were moments of transcendence — falling in love with Christ, receiving unconditional love from my grandmother, being out of my body — but that's not what I am speaking about. I'm speaking of something that occurs *consciously*. In the park that afternoon there was a conscious revelation of truth. I was on mescaline at the time, but psychedelics are no requirement. It can be as simple as watching, in full awareness, as a leaf falls from a tree.

On an acid trip I experienced the beauty of my

mother, the beauty of her freedom. I realized that her unbridled quality was what had given me the courage to take acid, to put the tab on my tongue. Her wildness was something I inherited from her. I had been trying to get rid of the wildness, to conform, for so long. In joining the counterculture I felt I was finally able to be myself, but that wasn't exactly true. It was more like that aspect of myself that was directly related to my mother and her absolute nonconformity could come out.

I felt a new compassion for her and her refusal to go along with the expectations of the South and our town and all the expectations that came with marrying the man she married. I admired her in some new, essential way. When I called her up and told her about that, she appreciated it.

But the psychedelics were hard on my nervous system. They intensified the hypersensitivity that had been present since I was a child, so I stopped taking them. Years later, when Ecstasy came out, before it was illegal, I was interested enough to try it. I loved the experiences I had on it. It was like a truth serum. I took it maybe five times, too. The last time, after the drug wore off, my eyes were stuck wide open. It was really awful! I couldn't close them. Luckily, that condition didn't last long. I don't think my nervous system will ever be the same after the Ecstasy.

The insights and revelations I had on psychedelics were wonderful, but the overriding teaching from them was this: If you are resisting something, you are in hell, and if you surrender, you are in bliss. I learned that from the psychedelics. As they would start to come on it was scary. I could feel the chemicals in my body and I'd think, "Oh my goodness, I've taken it. I've done it. I shouldn't have done this. What do I do now?!"

When I fought it like that it was a horrible experience, and it got worse and worse. But in a moment of, "Okay, it happened. It's here. It's in my system and it will last as long as it lasts," the experience instantly changed to, "Whoa, this is incredible!" That's primarily what I'm saying to people all the time now. If you just stop and experience this moment without resistance you see, "Oh. Bliss is here."

Sarah and I moved to Maui for about a year so I could live with the man I was involved with. When he and I separated I was lonely and made plans to return to California, but just before we left I decided to do a thirty-day training with Arica, an organization dedicated to personal transformation. By then I had seen that the external things I thought would make me happy, didn't. I was looking for some transcendental knowledge or personal revelation or enlightenment experience.

Just being a part of that Arica community was exciting. We did mantras, physical exercises, group processing of emotions, all in an intellectual framework that had a metaphysical bent. It was a very wild group, though. We met in an old mansion on a hill until, one day, the missionaries who rented it to us made a surprise visit. They found us thoroughly engaged, dancing naked in their living room!

At the time we were divorcing, Sarah's father got a second house in Bolinas, a small town on the coast. We were still good friends, and when Sarah and I got back to

California she lived there and went to school. I spent part of the time in Bolinas and then went back into San Francisco, and he would be there part of the time and then go to Berkeley where he worked.

Some followers of Swami Muktananda, an Indian guru who had a following in the States, were living in the house across the way. I had seen Muktananda when he came through Hawaii. I was part of a small group meeting with him, but I had no idea what was being offered. I was too busy looking for a date! It's funny, isn't it? Overlooking love while looking for a date?

Anyway, I became friendly with one of the people in the house who suggested that I meditate to help settle my nervous system. Using an egg timer, I began sitting for twenty minutes, twice a day. At first it was really hard because my mind was so all over the place. Simply not following the impulse to jump up and run was a challenge. I stuck with it for years, though, just sitting still, maybe watching my breath. It was settling. Once when I was meditating, the old childhood experience of my body disappearing came back, along with the fear: "Oh my God! Here it is! What if I am lost in this?" But since it came up while I was meditating, I knew not to run to find some medicine or someone to fix it. I knew to just stay here with whatever arises.

As a child I had refused to experience the fear of annihilation, so it was banished. There was a kind of spiritual fascism going on, a banishment of an aspect of myself. When I was meditating and in the context of the discovery of truth, it was: "I'm sitting here. I'm breathing. My body disappears. It disappears, and what is here is pure consciousness!" Then the actual experience of annihilation is bliss.

What I mean by "spiritual fascism" is the strategy we use when something comes up that we don't like in ourselves — maybe fear or some primal aggression—and rather than accepting it as part of the totality, we push it back into the dungeon of our subconscious. We deny it its existence by sending it off to the concentration camp.

The same neighbor who suggested I meditate was also a psychic. He told me that one day I would leave the area and when I came back I would be relatively famous, and that there would be something I would be doing where I would be looking into people's eyes. Isn't that amazing? I didn't know what he meant. I thought maybe he was talking about iridology, the study of the iris of the eye, so I tried that for a while. But that definitely wasn't it.

chapter seven

"FREE LOVE" HAD LOOKED so good watching "Woodstock," but then to be in the middle of it wasn't so good. By the mid-seventies I was starting to get jaded about the whole relationship thing. Maybe not jaded, but hopeless.

I never was interested in one-night stands. I was interested in intimate relationships, and I was getting discouraged about the possibility of finding a man who I could be with and love and respect, who would also support my discovery of truth. I wouldn't have phrased it that way at the time. I would have said it in a more feminist way, like "a man who would support my empowerment, who would let me be a powerful woman."

I'd stayed friends with the man Sarah and I had moved to Hawaii with. In 1975 he was visiting me in the city and he said, "Come to this party with me." He'd met a woman he was interested in having a relationship with, and her daughter was having a sixteenth birthday party. I said okay and we drove over to Berkeley.

My friend's new love interest was involved with another man at the time. His name was Eli. I think my friend and she wanted to set Eli and me up with each other so it would be easier for them to be together. When we were introduced at the party I thought Eli was nice, a real sweet guy, but that was all. I barely paid any attention to him. He was wearing these farm overalls and looked somewhat like a kid to me. That was our meeting.

I wasn't especially interested, but I went out with him a few times. There was a point when he came to see me in Bolinas. We were standing by a record player getting ready to put a record on. A light shot between us. We both went, "Wow! What was that?" I don't know what it was, maybe some electrical thing, but it looked like a ball of light. From that point on I felt and knew our relationship was huge, *is* huge.

He knew it, but in a different way. It took him a little while to understand it the way I did, that *this is a couple*. He knew it was big, but he was five years younger than me and didn't like the idea of settling down with one woman, whereas I was looking for a monogamous relationship.

I fell in love—passionately, deeply in love. It was such a surprise. He didn't fall in love with me immediately, so it was also a challenge. I was in love with this man who didn't fit any of my criteria for what the man I loved should look like or act like or be like. When I visualized my true love in my mind, he was some version of a blonde, Nordic god, not a New York Jewish hippie in overalls!

Then he fell in love. It was a partnership deeper than I'd even known could exist but was hungering for all the same, and he felt the same way. It satisfied a lot of our

needs because we both came from dysfunctional families. While we were satisfying each other at a certain level, something else deeper than that was also happening.

Eli was consciously on a spiritual search. I couldn't have said that about my first husband, even though he's a soulful being. Eli had had an awakening experience on psychedelics, an experience of himself as radiant consciousness. There was still a lot else going on with him, but he knew that that's what he wanted. He knew his life was devoted to that. Being with him was just what I needed. I feel so lucky to have met him. I don't know what would have happened if I hadn't. Maybe I would have continued just bouncing from one type of life to another.

The chemistry between us was very strong. I fell in

love with his intelligence and his humor, and he was introducing me to the possibility that one's whole life could be lived in the spiritual search. That's the way we would have said it then. We had a desire to learn how to stay high, to remain open and expansive, without taking drugs.

Much of our time together was spent either in nature or reading spiritual books. We were reading Lao Tsu, the *I Ching, The Secret of the Golden Flower.* I remember that the word "righteousness" was important. We talked a lot about being a righteous person, about how do we stop our greed and hatred and all that. It was thrilling! In Eli, I had finally met a match.

I was really happy, but that was the first year. Then the relationship went through a lot of unhappiness, too. It's never been a tranquil relationship, except maybe that first year.

We're very different types, Eli and I, and we're both strong personalities, so we've had lots of arguments. We've never been violent with each other, but we've definitely screamed at each other. We were immature when we got together, but whenever we started to split up one of us brought us back together. We didn't get far from each other, even though we hated each other at times, really hated each other.

Even now we have disagreements. Not the same kind, because there's such a different dynamic. Now we tend to bet. It's like, "Oh yeah, you wanna bet?" We can have silly arguments. Once I won some money driving back to Stinson Beach from Mendocino. He was saying we were

were in the Alexander Valley and I said, "No, we're not," because I'd just seen a sign naming it the Anderson Valley. So we bet and I won. We can definitely be irritated with one another.

There was a lot of fighting in my household growing up, so I don't mind it. It's not pleasant, of course, but I don't hold back from it. He also grew up in a household where they yelled at each other. I think one of the things that surprised him about me was that I wouldn't just walk away. I'd get in his face and we'd yell. There was a lot of passion because the fights were complicated by strong emotions like jealousy and fear. I'd jump out of the car at a stop sign, things like that.

Whenever we had a fight, or I found something about him I didn't like, I would imagine leaving, or finding someone else, or being on my own. Years later we came to a point where that stopped and I realized, "Oh, I'm going to stay in this relationship." So there was a whittling away at resistance, and my capacity for commitment kept deepening.

When Eli visited me in Bolinas he loved the funky little coastal town right away. He knew he wanted to live there. I decided to make the move with him and live there full time myself. I sold my wedding silver for probably a tenth of what it was worth to get enough money for two month's rent. We rented two separate bedrooms in a household. I roomed there with Eli and continued to stay at my ex-husband's house on the three or four nights a week that he was in Berkeley. By then I had gotten my massage therapy license. I left the waitressing-city-life and moved to Bolinas.

In the beginning marijuana was a big part of our relationship. Eli was growing it in Oregon, bringing it down
and selling it. It was an important part of his life and I
embraced it. I'd never smoked such good grass before. He
was like a missionary with it, preaching that if everybody
would just smoke, the whole world would be at peace. He
loved growing marijuana. It was his favorite thing. He
would probably be doing it right now, if he could.

In Bolinas we got interested in Tibetan Buddhism.
Our involvement was intense, though it didn't last long.
Kalu Rinpoche, the pre-eminent lama in the Kagyu
tradition, was coming to northern California and it was
decided he would visit Bolinas. There were some
Buddhists in our area. I don't think they were even
Tibetan Buddhists, but they were having an organizing
meeting to formally invite him to come to town. I went
to that meeting, thinking I might as well be a Buddhist as
anything.

Eli and I became part of a small group who worked
together to prepare a house for Rinpoche, scrubbing the
entire place and buying new bedding that no one had
ever slept on. Before he came we all took Bodhisattva
vows and got Tibetan names. Mine was White Tara, the
female embodiment of wisdom and compassion. Eli's was
Lion of Dharma.

When he arrived we were both struck by his serenity.
According to tradition, he was supposed to have a dream
that night to tell him who would be the new head of the
dharma center in Bolinas. He dreamed it would be Eli. I
would be something too. This really threw the people

who were in the group before us into a tizzy.

Possibly the whole event happened just for them. The man who was "the good student" flipped out because, after all, he had been there all along, and what did Rinpoche mean, "he dreamed of Eli"? Maybe he did dream about Eli. I don't know. Eli was clearly the alpha male of the group, and that's who the Tibetan Buddhists would want to represent them. They're a very wild bunch.

We set up a little Tibetan meditation center in our house. Every morning at five o'clock we would have a meditation, and then in the evening we'd have another one. I went to several Tibetan Buddhist retreats and they were beautiful in terms of the energy and the power of the monks' chanting. But still, it wasn't my thing. I was more attracted to Zen Buddhism because it was so clean. I loved the clarity of just sitting. It was what my nervous system needed. In the Tibetan practices I would get stirred up in a certain way, but it didn't feel healthy for this form to be into visualizations and magic and phenomenal events. So next we got involved with Zen.

chapter eight

IN 1977 ELI and I moved into my first husband's house in Bolinas and started living there with Sarah. We were part of a loose community of longhaired, nonviolent vegetarians. I got arrested for demonstrating against the Diablo Canyon Nuclear Power Plant and spent ten days in jail—sixteen of us women were in an eight-person cell—but my time there was more an adventure than a hardship.

For the most part Eli's and my life together was very simple. We didn't have a television. We didn't go to movies. We had a garden, some chickens and goats, and a horse for Sarah. Eli acted as my spiritual teacher, encouraging me to see what is really true. It was a healing time, but it wasn't without conflict.

Jealousy had been an issue for me my whole life. First, I was jealous of my sister because it seemed she really had my mother's love. I felt left out. Later, if a boyfriend was attracted to another girl, there'd be this cauldron of emotion. So by the time I entered the relationship with Eli the jealousy was very familiar. It was one of those jack-in-the-box issues. He was twenty-eight and interested in being with a lot of women. That was his political stance, what he believed in. I went along with him because I wanted to be with him, and I even thought he was right, but it was hard.

By the time I was consciously on a spiritual path a whole new set of "shoulds" had come into play, and I could see I was failing to live up to them. According to the new standard I was too yang, I "should" be more yin— or I was too possessive, I "should" be more yielding.

At that time there was a definite male-chauvinist bias to the whole counterculture. There was hardly any commitment from the men and many women were unhappy with that. We were supposed to be open and just let it be. Maybe the male animal is more able to have casual sex than the female. What I saw was women falling in love, which created suffering that wasn't being talked about, that was being pushed aside.

There was a cultural lie going on, with the spiritual overlay: "I shouldn't be jealous. If I'm jealous, that's my problem. It's only because I'm not evolved enough to open my heart to all beings." A lot of personal clearing had to take place before I even had a clue what was happening. Plus, I had some affairs of my own during our relationship. I was looking for pleasure, but primarily I wanted to avoid the heartbreak of Eli not being true.

Luckily, I ran into co-counseling, which is called peer counseling now. You do peer counseling in a pair with another layperson. You're trained to take turns listening to your partner without giving advice or trying to fix them.

Peer counseling really supports telling the truth. In that environment I expressed how I felt and accepted what was there. If you're jealous, you're jealous, and so you ask, "What does that feel like?" I had been lying to myself about my emotions because I'd decided they weren't spiritual. I wasn't overtly lying, but I was lying as we do in repression and denial.

Years later, once I released the emotions of anger, fear and despair connected to the jealousy, I discovered clarity under them. This led me to say, "Eli, if you want to do this, fine, but I'm not interested in having an open relationship anymore."

On that day I was home alone, and my personal mantra began: "Oh, what is happening in this relationship? Is Eli being true to me or is he having other affairs? If he is having other affairs, does that really threaten me? What will happen?"

At last, I asked myself unsentimentally, "What do I really want?" I could see how I was using my life force, and it was clear I no longer wanted my life to revolve around the state of the relationship and the self-torture I inflicted on myself about it. I knew, without a doubt, that I had had enough. If it meant I would live the rest of my life without relationship, then so be it.

Eli often talks about how once I got clear and spoke to him clearly, he understood. By then we were studying the enneagram, which led us to a lot of important insights. (I'll tell more about that later.) Eli says when he saw I was willing to lose the whole relationship—that there was something bigger to me than our contract— that's when I became his teacher. At that point, our roles switched.

In Bolinas I worked as a massage therapist for a while, but it was tough. Everything I tried to do was so hard on my body. I remember how it shocked people in Mississippi when they heard I was doing massage therapy, which just meant prostitution to them. For me, I loved the way the massage could be intimate without being sexual, but because of something to do with my sensitive constitution, I took on the energy of my clients. Often I felt wiped out and out of balance, which Western medicine doesn't address.

I began seeing a wonderful local acupuncturist who helped me. Unexpectedly, I discovered the euphoria of energetic alignment. It was natural to ask myself if I could switch from massage therapy to acupuncture, because I wanted to share what I received, and I figured I wouldn't take on so much of other people's energy if I didn't have to touch them.

In those days there was no place around to study acupuncture. My acupuncturist's teacher happened to be in England, so I went to train with him there. I was in Lemmington, England, for six weeks with my class of Americans. Then the next year we went back for testing and more instruction. After that a center opened in Maryland and I saw my teacher there.

I loved the training. It helped restructure my thought process about the way the world works. Acupuncture is Eastern and circular, rather than linear. There has to be something that changes your world view. For a man I met while visiting a federal penitentiary, it was years in prison and recognizing the failure of his life. Psychedelics changed the way I saw things, but acupuncture is very sober, and it still shows the same kind of depth of reality and mystery.

When my teacher was showing us how to read the pulses, how to find a point and what energy to bring into the point, over and over he would repeat, "Just get out of the way. Just get yourself out of the way." I can't say I knew what he meant, but it sank in anyway.

When I read pulses I had to stop my thought process. I had to just be there with the pulse. When you stop thinking, there is a kind of life that is experienced. It is the same with acupuncture points. If you are just there with them, communication occurs that doesn't make sense to a Western mind. It's a non-material meeting that is awesome to discover. The possibility that you can actually communicate with the lungs and the heart—that they're alive, that they're living entities and not just pieces of meat with electrical impulses going through them—had a huge influence on me.

Sarah was twelve and going into puberty when I began studying acupuncture. She was having a difficult time. One day I came home from interning and she had some friends over. She'd had kissing parties at our house before, but this get-together was different from a kissing party. It was a making-out party. She had been making out. I could see it all over her. Her hormones had kicked in, and I saw there was danger of something happening way too soon.

I thought, "Well, she could be miserable all her life if

she follows this," so that day I called her father. He came the next morning to pick her up and move her to Berkeley to live with him and his new wife.

Sarah was furious with me. She had this boyfriend and had just awakened to what a real kiss is, what a real kiss feels like. Once again I was separating her from what felt good. Her horse and friends were in Bolinas and she was losing all that.

I used the episode as a way to beat myself up. "I gave up my daughter! I gave up my child! Isn't this proof that I really am the worst of the worst?" I would just be racked with sobs. I knew it was the best thing for her, but I still had emotional attachments. I wanted to be with her. I wanted to be a good mother and prove to myself that I could be a good mother. But I was not a good mother, and once I started learning acupuncture I had to be away and have time to study. She needed a firmer hand.

A few years after she moved in with her father, Eli and I did EST, a personal transformation training. We got my first husband, his new wife, and Sarah to do it, too. Sarah was in an adult group somehow, and she loved it. Around that time I took her out for lunch, to tell her how sorry I was about all the mistakes I'd made as her mother. I told her, "Listen, I am sorry. I am *really* sorry." I had a lot to be sorry for. I had been so involved with my drama—*my* suffering, what *I* needed, what *I* wasn't getting, and what *she* wasn't giving me. She said something like, "Mom, you keep apologizing." I guess it wasn't the first time, but it was the first time I remember. She added, "It's really over."

Sitting across the table from her in the crowded cafe there was a moment when I could truly see her. What I saw was so pure and untouched by any of my desires. She caught that. In the instant she saw me seeing her I said, "I see you for the first time. I have never really seen you before." A spark of true recognition passed between us.

Until the late seventies Eli and I were making an invisible, counter-cultural income. He was still growing marijuana, and we barely spent any money. When I wanted to become an acupuncturist he financed it from a really nice crop he grew. The next year he grew another crop but the sheriff came and ripped it out. Even though Eli didn't get arrested it was clear his grass-growing days were over. He didn't know what to do. That's about the time that the counter-culture ended, and for many of us it was "what to do?" The dreams of Utopia, of all just hanging out together, were over.

Around then Eli happened upon neurolinguistic pro-gramming and Ericksonian Hypnosis, which he studied in Santa Cruz. Neurolinguistic programming, or NLP, is a therapeutic intervention that changes the way we structure internal reality through changing our use of language. Eli had an affinity for it and became an NLP counselor.

During the years when he was leading NLP groups we traveled to Japan a couple of times. We went to a Zen temple in Beppu where Eli knew the head priest. They'd done psychedelics together in the sixties, and his friend had been unexpectedly summoned back to Japan to take charge of a family-run temple. We were able to bring groups to this ancient, beautiful place for meditation and nontraditional workshops.

When I discovered Zen Buddhism I made Japan the ideal. I was infatuated with its sense of aesthetics and its exquisite representation of the Zen moment. I believed that if I dressed in the "Zen" style and made my environment more "Zen," if I adopted the Eastern point of view, then I would be who I wanted to be.

I remember my surprise when I finally got to Japan and saw what it was really like—women trying to get liberated from being subservient, men trying to gain status through accumulation. They were all trying to be like us! I became disillusioned with my tendency to romanticize "the other" in the hope "the other" would give me what I wanted. Disillusionment has been a very useful state in this life. Through it I've discovered that imitation cannot deliver what is authentic.

My acupuncture practice was immediately rewarding, even though it was challenging at first. You can't really know anything until you start practicing, and I was learning so much so quickly. It was new then, before there were many acupuncturists.

I was taking classes to learn Chinese herbal medicine. Eli and I had a great t'ai chi teacher in Berkeley, and we began learning Chinese. We were swept up in the romance of it all.

The t'ai chi was good, and it was something I enjoyed sharing with Eli, but dancing was always more meaningful to me. As a little girl I had studied ballet and I danced a lot in high school. It was early rock-and-roll then. What I loved was being able to really, *really* let go. As a quasi-hippie I did this wild, free-form dancing. It was a way of discharging stored-up energy. My body liked it and it was great exercise. I always saw myself as a dancer, or a wannabe dancer, or a could-have-been dancer. After the t'ai chi I did some movement work with an excellent teacher. This prepared me to teach movement classes to Eli's groups, the ones we took to Japan and those he did at Esalen.

Eli and I were both lucky, lucky, lucky. I had found acupuncture, which I loved and which turned out to be lucrative, and Eli had found NLP. After a couple of years we moved out of sleepy little Bolinas into bustling Mill Valley, somehow slipping back into the mainstream. We opened a clinic in a good location in San Francisco and began commuting. Eli did NLP counseling. I did acupunctures. There was someone else in our office doing

WITH SARAH BACK IN CLARKSDALE

massage, and it was good. Slowly we became legitimate and bought a wonderful little house in Mill Valley.

The Taoist understanding I adopted is very grounded in the body. Our t'ai chi teacher was in his fifties and proud he could still move around like a monkey. The ideal is to live to be one hundred in perfect health. It was exciting for me to think that I could reach a state of perfect health. There was a sign in the office of the acupuncturist I went to see that read "Health Is Freedom."

My life was very busy. I was either giving acupuncture treatments or receiving them or studying about them. Along with t'ai chi, and then dance, and the classes in herbal medicine and Chinese, I became an examiner for people testing to get their acupuncture licenses and a mentor to prospective acupuncturists. Eli and I often worked late and ate out. Then I'd study from the huge books I brought home almost every night and wouldn't get to bed until after midnight. I loved it. It suited my type A personality.

But I was still searching. In my practice I was treating some Vipassana teachers I liked, so I decided to check out Vipassana. I did a ten-day retreat at Joshua Tree in the desert near Palm Springs. We were instructed to sit without physically moving, which was a new level of not moving for me. If you got an itch, you weren't supposed to scratch.

We would sit for forty-five minutes, and walk for forty-five minutes, then sit for forty-five minutes, and walk for forty-five minutes, have a little lunch, sit for forty-five minutes, and walk for forty-five minutes, all

LEAVING FOR WORK

through the day, from six in the morning until eight at
night. There would be a couple of short, beautiful
Buddhist talks each day.

The retreat reinforced the possibility of not following
my thoughts. When I began to sit, right away there would
be physical pain. Even though I was limber, all of a sudden my knees were killing me. So I thought, "Obviously
this is very dangerous for my body." Then I had to go to
the bathroom. So: "This is unhealthy and my bladder
might burst." Then: "I have to open my eyes because
surely the teacher has missed the time. Surely it has been

more than forty-five minutes. Is he asleep? Did he die?" And those were just the gross thoughts. It could get very subtle.

Sitting gave me an opportunity to be there with whatever came up, to not move physically, and to not entertain the thought, "Oh, now I'm not moving. That means I'm holy."

Vipassana is always about sitting. I had a powerful experience on the retreat. When I spoke to one of the teachers who I'd guessed had similar experiences because he'd been a serious meditator for years, he couldn't, or wouldn't, truly meet me in it. That was so different from my teacher, Papaji, who, when I finally found him, would meet me in any experience. I didn't do another retreat, but sitting felt refreshing and healthy. I respected this and continued the meditation on my own.

chapter nine

IN 1983 A GOOD FRIEND of ours got involved with the enneagram and suggested we invite a teacher to give a workshop at our house, which we did. We both loved it immediately as a way to see our own stuff. The enneagram is a wisdom tradition that exposes nine essential ways in which consciousness identifies or fixates itself as ego. Each ego fixation is numbered, one through nine. Eli saw it as a deeper transformational pathway than any he'd encountered and eventually began offering enneagram workshops himself.

The enneagram can be extremely helpful in seeing that one's patterns aren't personal. Until then I couldn't believe I had such negative thoughts about myself and other people. It was a relief to see that everyone has them, and that they are more a matter of habit—a groove that one keeps slipping into—than proof of how bad one is.

Right away I saw how big a part of my fixation the jealousy was. It wasn't necessarily just a law of nature. Maybe it is a law of nature at a certain level, but the way it was played out, the twisting and turning of the knife, was really my fixation. I got to see myself as "a four" in the enneagram—Miss Drama Queen, somebody who believes: "Nobody suffers like I do."

Seeing my family dynamic from the point of view of the enneagram was immensely useful. My mother was "an eight," and a hedonistic eight. Eights are the bullies of the enneagram who justify their anger. I saw her anger really had nothing to do with me—or, in a sense, with her.

What a dynamic to become aware of! I'm born here with this "eight" mother and a "nine" father, who typically goes along with his partner to avoid conflict, and I am the drama queen who takes everything personally.

Along with learning the enneagram came a real willingness to see what was primally driving the jealousy. It was a true investigation. As a story, I traced the jealousy back to what I felt after the birth of my sister. But when I met the jealousy emotionally, there was a fear of isolation under it. And under that was this sense of actual unworthiness—that sooner or later I would be discarded for another. Being sent away to the preventorium when I was six had crystallized that fear. I saw that the internalization of unworthiness was what was driving the jealousy.

In this investigation I was willing to experience the ugliness of unworthiness. Years before, the therapist in San Francisco had directed me to go deeply into some feeling I was having, and I experienced myself as a burned, black gnarl. I had burnt my hand very badly when I was five and that image was still in place. I was terribly ashamed about burning my hand. For decades it was my shame. My father's mother had a young maid who must have been thirteen or fourteen years old—a child, really. She was ironing and was supposed to be watching me while my mother and grandmother visited in another room. I asked her if I could iron and she said, "Sure," and showed me how. Then she left the room. The iron was called a "mangle." It was one of those old-fashioned roller irons for sheets, and when I was smoothing out the sheet, it caught my hand. Whew! She had told me what all the buttons meant and the only one I could remember, thank God, was the one to stop it. My hand was badly damaged and I had to have multiple operations on it. I was left with an ugly scar. To me it seemed like the scar reflected what was inside me, a deep grossness that the normal skin usually covers.

The jealousy was really a protection against meeting this worthless, already discarded thing. Then, going even deeper, I met the black hole underneath that. After I met Papaji, it was incredible and wonderful to see how the way we were using the enneagram merged with his teacher Ramana's inquiry into meeting death. I realized it was the same investigation: *Who am I?*

It was liberating. I met the jealousy that drove me and recognized how it was protecting me from something deeper in the subconscious that was even worse than jealousy. There was freedom in directly experiencing worthlessness and discovering it to be nothing at all.

So, after years of investigation, jealousy ended. Well, who knows if it's ended? I don't like to say anything's ended. Let's not tempt the gods here. And I don't know that jealousy has to end. I wouldn't make anything having to end be a condition of awakening, because everything that's here is potentially a vehicle for discovering what's underneath it all.

In 1985 my mother died from lung cancer. For most of my life I had seen her as some demon out to torture me—an advanced, powerful being determined to make my life miserable.

By the time of her death I understood that she hadn't really intended me harm. She was simply playing out her destiny, and if that play created suffering for me, then that's what happened.

When I went to visit her in the last weeks of her life, I was able to just be with her without needing her to express her love for me or be different in any way. When true acceptance is there anybody can feel it, and she understood. My mother was always funny and she said, in this I-told-you-so voice, "Well, finally!" And I said, "Yeah, it took me awhile." So it ended really well.

Years earlier I'd had a surprising experience. I'd called her on the phone one Mother's Day. By then I'd had a lot of space from her, and she was old and sick. That day I thought, "I am feeling oceanic. I will call her and I'll just lie to her. I'll say, 'You were a great mother.' I'll lie. So what?"

So I called her and said, "Mama, you know what? You were a great mother." And as the words came out of my mouth, they were true! What a relief! It didn't mean she did great things. It didn't mean her intentions were always great. But I saw that the wholeness of my life experience was ultimately augmented by my relationship with this very difficult woman.

I had no idea what the effect of saying those words would be, but at the moment I said them, the grudge I always had against her—and against myself and against life for my not being able to win her—was erased.

Our clinic was going strong but I began to experience major burn-out. I was seeing too many people and not getting the rest I needed. There were a lot of draining aspects to our lives that were going unnoticed.

We were eating out every night because we were working so much that neither one of us had time to cook. I was taking a very intense dance class in the mornings in Marin. From there I would drive into the city to work. We had a huge mortgage to pay, so there was money pressure.

I was overdoing it, but I had no idea my body was collapsing under me. It was a last burst of thinking that there is endless physical energy, when actually I was past forty and starting the downhill slope. Because I liked my work so much, the burn-out snuck up on me.

By the spring of 1988 I couldn't continue. One day I was treating somebody and I sort of lurched in the treatment room. The next morning I couldn't get out of bed. I asked myself, "What? Why can't I get up and do my work?" But I was too physically spent. I just could not move my body.

Eli was great. He told me it didn't matter if I had to stay in bed for the rest of my life. He said to just relax, it would be fine. When I did relax it became clear I was too exhausted to even try to go back to work. In finally acknowledging that, I started to hear the birds sing again. They were just outside my bedroom window, but I hadn't heard them for a long time.

"What have I been doing?" I asked. "I've been going full speed." I had to realize while there is an adrenaline rush in that, it also creates an adrenaline depletion, and I had reached my limit.

chapter ten

ELI AND I BOTH BEGAN to ask, "What have we done?"
We'd avoided the mainstream in the first place because of
its focus on the material. Yet there we were, back in the
fast life—working, working, working to support our
lifestyle. We had to look honestly at what we were doing.

After years of the country life it had been great fun to
dress ourselves up, go to fine restaurants, enjoy the food
and wine. We'd done a lot of that, but that was not what
we got together for, and we were not fulfilled. What I
learned from the acupuncture was immense, and Eli had
founded Pacific Center for Sacred Studies which spon-
sored the enneagram teachings we'd attended and those
he'd taught. So Mill Valley had been a rich and exciting
time, but we weren't truly satisfied.

Our yuppie days were over. Maybe it was good to do
it, to play out that role, so there could be a recognition
that "the good life" is not enough.

I began asking the Universe for help and I felt that we
were being guided to leave Marin. As it got more and
more crowded in Mill Valley there was a big upswing in
the real estate market so we were able to sell our house
at a substantial profit. We decided to move to Hawaii

with the idea of eventually opening a Pacific Center for Sacred Studies there. Eli was still teaching neurolinguistic programming and Ericksonian Hypnosis at Esalen and offering enneagram workshops, but I wasn't doing anything.

We'd visited Maui a couple of times together and had a strong spiritual connection there. We felt the spirit of the island through powerful experiences in the ocean and the volcano, and in the village of Hana. Aside from the power of the ocean and the land, in those days it was very slow in Maui. When things are slow there can be a recognition of the Presence that is easily overlooked when things speed up.

We moved there in late 1988 and rented an old house on a farm owned by a Japanese American family. It had huge avocado trees, persimmons, and an abundance of

flowers. We were so excited because by seven in the evening there was nobody on the roads. We thought that was wonderful—the peace and quiet, and the beauty of the place. Our lives were good, better than ever.

Eli and I got married. We already knew we were life partners, so a lot of the ceremony was a declaration

to the world. Eli was teaching and traveling, and I was traveling with him, sometimes teaching dance. We were happy to say, "We are married. We are husband and wife."

We had two weddings. First we were married in a church, which covered the legal aspect. Then, within a few days, we married ourselves in a cave in Haleakala volcano. The cave marriage was more representative of who we were at that time. During the ceremony we reaffirmed that our bond was centered on the discovery of truth— truth as the priority of the relationship, and coming before the relationship.

There was an intense storm that day and very few of the people who planned to hike in with us made it. After we said our vows we were all in a little cabin right by the cave, soaking wet. Unexpectedly, a very large man who we didn't even know showed up with a bottle of thirty-year-old cognac. He arrived on a mule wearing a heavy oil slicker. He called himself "German John," and told us he'd been trained by the Kahunas and just felt drawn to be there.

We all formed a circle and he led us in a beautiful marriage toast. It was one of those magical moments. Later, we had a huge party at one of the local mansions.

It was wonderful living in Maui, sort of the opposite of living in Marin, and life went very well, but something was still missing. There were moments of perfect contentment and bliss, but then, as circumstances would change, I'd feel the same tightness or knot. There was still an underlying tension, something not yet resolved. There was some kind of unanswered question, along with looking for what the next moment would bring.

I had a strong desire to keep what happiness I had and to keep away any misery that might possibly come in. That, in itself, is suffering.

I had tried so many things to find lasting happiness, more than I've mentioned here. I had spent many years in the search. I really didn't know what to do anymore. I'd dealt with a lot of my neuroses, and certainly there was more light in my life.

I no longer had the sense of myself as this ugly, miserable creature. I knew that I was living a lucky life. I had

had the pleasure of a successful career and the delight of a successful relationship, and though I hadn't been a success in raising my daughter, she turned out great, so I was lucky there too.

But even though I was quite self-assured, and had many experiences of unity and cosmic consciousness, which was what I wanted, there was always re-identification with myself as a sufferer. However great the experience, however great the appearance of Oneness, it would be conceptualized and put in my mind.

So I had to tell the truth and acknowledge that there was something missing—some essential, elusive, missing piece. Out of that I prayed for a teacher.

I had never wanted a teacher before. I'd wanted *teachings,* and teachers who could give me the teachings, but not *a teacher.* Finally I cried out for a true teacher. "I can't do it by myself. I want a living, breathing teacher, a final teacher, somebody to cut this knot." Even if a true teacher would reveal there is no safety, no happiness, and that the possibility of enlightenment is all a lie, I wanted to know that. I made the deepest prayer of my life for help.

Occasionally we went back to the Bay Area for Eli's work. When we were there a friend said, "I went to see an American teacher who says he is enlightened. Let's go, I think you'd like him."

When I met him I was very impressed. He was somebody like us, and yet he had absolute confidence in what he was saying. This got my attention. All of the other spiritual teachers I'd met were either from Tibet or Japan or someplace else. They were removed, not speaking my vernacular. This man was willing to address whatever was brought up in my language. I got Eli to come see him and he was quite excited too. He said, "This proves it. It is possible. If he can do it, I can do it. You can do it."

I made arrangements with a friend who was also living on Maui to sit with this man for a month in California. I wanted Eli to come, but he was making other plans. He was going to Sikkim to find a Tibetan teacher, and to Pakistan to search for Sufis. I was sure he was making a big mistake, going through some kind of a mid-life crisis, but he was on his way.

This story is really Eli's, but I'll tell parts of it. He had to stop in Delhi to get his visa. While in Delhi, he met a government official who claimed to know some enlightened Sufis. Eli went to Lucknow, where the official lived, to get their names. When he got to Lucknow, Eli remembered that the man I was sitting with had been with a guru from Lucknow, so he called me and told me to ask him for this Indian guru's name.

I asked him, but he refused to give me the name. Eli really wanted to find this Indian master and he didn't know what to do. Then I found the book this American teacher had written. In it he talked about his guru and named him. I got back to Eli to tell him the man he was looking for was H.W.L. Poonja.

Eli looked in the phone book under "Poonja" but there were several "Poonjas" listed. He wandered up to the top of his hotel, the Carleton, in the old part of the city. While praying there he saw two Indian kites. In fact, he didn't know they were kites. He didn't know what he was seeing. He thought they might be birds playing with each other, he wasn't sure, but he took whatever it was to be a sign. He made his way to that spot in a downtown Lucknow neighborhood. When he got there he asked some people if they knew a Sri Poonja. They did and gave him directions to a little house where he lived with his family.

Eli knocked on the door and was surprised when a very kind-looking man, Papaji's son, answered and said, "Please come in. He is waiting for you."

Eli walked into a tiny bedroom. He and Papaji met. They just fell in love. Papaji—that's what Eli called him because that's what he was called by his grandchildren— had only just gotten back from being at the hospital with some complication from diabetes. He was at home recovering.

Eli got to spend five days all alone with him in his room, every day, and they were in bliss. He would write me these letters that were *alive!* When I received them they would be vibrating with sublime samadhi.

And that is what brought me to Papaji.

PAPAJI

chapter eleven

I HAD NEVER WANTED a guru. I thought I was beyond that. Besides, I'd seen too much potential for abuse and co-dependency in the guru-disciple relationship. As a liberated American woman I thought I was too sophisticated, that I knew way too much. But a few months earlier, when I prayed for a teacher, some arrogant stance dropped away. I had truly given up, and with that I'd accepted that I couldn't figure things out on my own. I no longer had any idea of what the answer to my prayer *should* look like.

After spending a month with Papaji, Eli returned to Maui changed. He was transmitting silence. Then, in April of 1990, we went to India together. He wanted to introduce me to Papaji, and I wanted to meet him. Eli bought tickets for the same friend I'd gone to Marin with to sit with Papaji's disciple, and for her son, so we all could go.

Papaji wasn't in Lucknow then. He was in Hardwar where he rented a house during the hot season, and by April it was already hot in Lucknow. Hardwar was in the hills, on the bank of the River Ganga. Papaji would usually meet with some people at his house in the morning and then invite a few of them to come back in the afternoon. We arrived in the afternoon, just showed up at his house and knocked on the door. I think there were a couple of French women inside having tea.

Papaji opened the door. There he was, a large Punjabi man with this huge welcome, this open smile and these brilliant eyes. His eyes were ablaze with the welcome. Then I knew: *This is better than I could have imagined.* I was really speechless at his beauty and the love he was offering, unconditionally, without checking me out to see if I was worthy or if I would make good use of it—just offering it. I knew he was the teacher I had been asking for. So it was a very joyous moment and a very serious moment.

For me, meeting Papaji was the decisive moment. There were great realizations and insights afterward, but it

was the *meeting* of Papaji that all of the rest came from. That was the moment of surrender.

Papaji's American disciple had talked to his own students a lot about their responsibility to him. I deeply appreciate him for that because it prepared me to pay very close attention to Papaji. Having found my teacher, I knew that it was up to me. I had to give all my attention to him and see where that took me.

Eli and I were with Papaji for six weeks, seeing him every day. We stayed in a government guest house across the river from his place. We could see his balcony from our room. To get to his house we had to cross the river on a bridge. Each day we would pass a lady who made malas out of roses and we'd buy one for Papaji to place around his neck. Then we'd walk up to his place where we met in a sky-blue room.

The room was small, with peeling walls and heavy mold in the corners. It was a place that would have been disgusting before, but because Papaji was there, it was beautiful, shining with the radiance of his being. Papaji's son, Surendra, was staying with him, taking care of him and making sure he ate. In the satsang room you could hear the steam pots and the pressure cookers from his kitchen. The sounds from the street drifted into the room. Right out the front door the River Ganga was wild and rushing and an intense green color. I had never experienced anything like it. It was starting to get very hot. There were beggars and flies and getting sick from the food. And always this thread of the sublime purpose of being there.

WHERE PAPAJI STAYED IN HARDWAR

From the first, I felt no distance from Papaji. I recognized him as the parent I had wanted all those lonely days and nights in Mississippi. He even looked like my father to me. And he felt so like my papa, instructing me in the most essential way. He was offering me what my parents were ill-equipped to offer. No one had offered it to them, and they hadn't had the inclination to find it.

We were lucky because Papaji was very available, working closely with the people who came to see him. In

satsang there were fifteen of us at the most. Every morning he would ask us each for a little report. It was
wonderful to have so much of his individual attention, but
I don't think being in a small group was critical. I would
definitely say that the essential thing was that I met him,
not when or how. I trust that if I had met him three years
later in a horde of people, I would have had the same
recognition and the same resolve to listen to him. Even
though I met him in India, Papaji's message is not Indian.
It is not Hindu, though he happened to have been
brought up as a Hindu. His message is not bound to any
culture.

He says the truth of who you are, right now, is already
free. The truth of who you are is already at peace. The
truth of who you are, at this moment, is already in bliss,
in fulfillment. There is no need to search for anything
because you already *are* everything you are looking for. It
is only the distraction of mind that keeps you from recognizing it.

When I heard this teaching from him I asked,
"How? How do I get what you have? I want to know
that." He answered, "It is very easy. All you have to do is,
for one moment, stop. Stop trying to get anything. Stop
every technique, every strategy of your mind to acquire
anything."

I heard this, and at one level I understood. "Oh, okay.
I will stop. He means relax. Okay." But in that stopping a
deeper activity of mind was revealed: "Yes, but if I really
stop trying to get what he has, then maybe I will never
get it, and maybe I will lose what I already have." And he
said, "Stop that."

I thought, "What he is saying is too simple. It's too easy. I have got to work on myself, I have got to do more." I did not realize it was terror that was driving that thought, but it was. There was terror that I would not get to perfect this image of myself, and there had been a lot of time and energy invested in creating it. It had seemed to me that there had been some payoff too, some progress. I definitely was not as miserable as I had been in the fourth grade, or as a young adult. And so when Papaji said to stop, there was fear that I would lose all that I had gained.

With that there was an even deeper thought: "I have to have this image of myself so that it can enjoy the awakening of myself." I had spent many moments of every day supporting, maintaining, practicing, and actually worshipping this image of myself.

Papaji was not talking about killing it, because how do you kill an image? It was recognizing, "This is an image of myself, and it only continues if I continue the practice and the fabrication and the worship of it. It takes effort to maintain it, and the effort has been going on for so long that it seems natural."

What I had heard from teachers before was, "Take this belief. Take this idea. Get rid of those ideas and take this one. Take this religion. Forget your old religion and take this religion. Take this style. Take this form of meditation. Take this thought form." But it was clear Papaji was not saying any of that. And he wasn't asking me to be still as in a stupor, nor to stop as in denial. He was saying, "Stop.

Stop it all. Be still. Be still as inquiry, the investigating force, which is Consciousness inquiring into Itself. Call off the search. Inquire into who you are."

What a shock! All of the momentum had been to continue the search, and to search more, and to search harder, and to search more thoroughly, and harder and harder and harder. To hear this "Stop!" was huge. It shook my whole universe. I understood that everything was threatened, all the artificial me's I had created throughout my life. "Oh, well, I am a woman." "Oh, I am a woman with a mate." "Oh, I am a woman who lost a mate." "Oh, I am a woman who, even though she lost a mate, found another mate." All these self-definitions had been some kind of security to fall back on, some kind of escape. But when he said stop *everything*, I really heard him.

He was telling me that the way to discover my true self, my *Self*, is to drop every idea of myself, including every idea of success and every idea of failure. This stopping didn't allow for my successes in finding a brighter, shinier me. Even my most recent success in finding him, as sweet as it was, was included in what had to stop. "Stop everything. Really stop."

It's possible others had said this to me. But I listened to him as I had never listened to anyone, because he had a certain power, because I was at the end of my rope, and because he had been the answer to a prayer. So even though reasons came up not to stop, I said to myself, "Well, why not? I will stop. I will stop right here. If the body dies, so be it. If I lose all that I have gained in my idea of what spiritual attainment is, so be it. If I am taken advantage of or seen as a fool, so be it." And in that willingness, in that moment, there was a recognition of that which is completely independent of who I think I am, a recognition of that which is always present, always radiant, always at peace.

When I was with Papaji I often went into bliss. I had no idea I existed. But he would not let me stay there very long. He had seen that with spiritual seekers in general there can be a heavy addiction to the bliss state, as if it is the truth of who one is. Bliss is a beautiful state. It is a high state, much higher than the depressive states. But if you are addicted to heaven, it is hell.

That is what he said to us, and it is the truth. There has to be a real willingness to see this truth. He would tell us stories about people who were able to sustain states for thirty, forty, fifty years. But his view was, "So what? That is still not the truth of who you are. It is still a state. Whatever is here that was not here before will be gone sometime."

Over and over Papaji reminded us to let our attention rest on the eternal. I remember once, a few years after we met, I wrote him about some gossip that was happening about me and I asked, "Papaji, what should I do about this?" He answered, "If your attention is on that gossip, how can your attention be on the Beloved?"

It is so simple. At first I struggled with what he was asking me to examine and inquire into, but I just gave myself to it until, mysteriously, there was a pop, and then there was understanding.

In those early days I tried to use my strategies on him. He didn't like it. First I tried to be really holy. I have always spent a lot of time on how I look. I took off all my makeup and dressed down, trying to look like I thought a holy person would. I think I didn't even brush my hair. After a couple of days of that he said, "Whew, go fix yourself up!" Next I tried to be very independent, acting like, "Oh, well, the guru and I are one, so, 'Hey, Papaji, how are you doing?'" He couldn't tolerate me. Then I fell into an old tactic of being oh so humble, striking kind of a meek, imploring attitude. "Oh Papaji, Papaji, Papaji," and he went, "Whoa!"

It wasn't that he ever said anything negative to me. All he had to do was raise his eyebrow and I knew he was not pleased. It was perfect that he saw my absurdities, because in his seeing I saw what I had no idea was there. I got to see the face of my personality which I had thought was covered by some learned way to be. Finally I got it. "Oh, I see. There is no right way to play this. There is no right way that this looks."

In the years since then I've seen that to whatever degree we hold ourselves back because of what we think we should be doing, or what we think someone else thinks we should be doing—however much we hold back the essence of our being—to that degree we cannot receive the essence of All Being.

I remember how Eli, Yamuna, our dear friend, and I would just sit around our room together and say, "I am the happiest person in the world." "No, no. *I* am the happiest person in the world." "But *I* am the happiest person

in the world." This happiness, "the happiest in the world,"
is one's nature that is released as the facade of the personality cracks and crumbles.

chapter twelve

PAPAJI HAD A huge stride. In the afternoons we would go on walks with him in the marketplace of Hardwar. This was just as his feet were starting to deteriorate from diabetes and he was intent on walking, trying to keep the body going. In the market there was a man with a scale whom you could pay to weigh you, and Papaji was unabashedly proud when his weight was low. He was just so lovable. I was falling deeply in love with him. I could feel my whole being opening.

On one of our walks I was behind him and all of a sudden doubt about the whole thing came up. "Is this all hocus-pocus? Is this all superstition? This could not be true. What about Christ? If I follow this teacher I will burn eternally in Hell!" I did not know what was true. How could I? I had just met him. Maybe he was just on some kind of power trip. Maybe he was going to take all of my money or make me be a part of a group marriage. For all I knew this questioning was the voice of inner wisdom.

In that moment it was clear there was a choice that had to be made. My choice was, "Well, all right. I feel this Grace, and I have never been touched like this before. There is something here that my mind cannot get hold of. Instead of following the doubt into some kind of sophisticated, cynical argument about co-dependency and neurosis and all the rest, I will stop. I will just stop, be still and see."

I saw that any time this obsessive kind of questioning comes up, it's a kind of agitation of the mind that really doesn't lead to clarity; it just leads to more agitation. The possibility is to be still and see. Then, if this whole thing is just some further neurotic play, it will become apparent. I was willing to trust that if Papaji was a charlatan, and this was all just his sideshow, it would become obvious. That was a great moment because then I wasn't so terrorized by my mind, or its doubting capacity, or its cynicism. I could just wait and see.

The marketplace was noisy, dirty and smelly, with people grabbing and pushing. On our first walks I wondered, "How could Papaji bring us here?" I had come from so far, and being in his little room in satsang was heaven to me. Now he was taking me out into hell.

One afternoon, as I was walking through the market stalls, I stopped clinging to being "in satsang" in his room. I stopped resisting the sights and sounds around me. With the letting-go came the recognition that the pristine awareness I was longing for, that I'd discovered in satsang, hadn't gone anywhere. How could it?

In fact, it was the other way around. It was I who'd left it, or, more accurately, my attention had. The silence was everywhere, just underneath the sounds. The beauty, under the sights, radiated through them. The boundary between the marketplace and Papaji's room was revealed to be imaginary. It was the same see-er seeing both. *I am Consciousness—radiant, alive and unchanging.*

I've often been asked about the role of the guru. In my life it took a living guru who could look me in the eye and speak the truth for me to trust enough to hear. It's like the way it is with an animal. You can't heal a wounded animal until that animal lets you come close.

When I was five years old I was bitten by a dog. I saw a neighborhood dog hit by a car. I'd never had any experience with animals except as playmates so I ran out to help him, and he bit me. I was shocked. My mother explained that the dog was so scared and hurt that he thought I was going to hurt him some more.

The same thing is demonstrated in the movie "The Horse Whisperer." A horse who had been badly injured wouldn't let the girl who'd always loved him near. None of the people who knew him could get close. It took a special person who could get on the wavelength of the horse and speak to it energetically for the horse to trust again. On a tantric level, what happened between Papaji and me was like that. My underlying negativity was the reflection of deep wounds, and it took his unconditional love to melt my resistance and turn me around.

Papaji was not a traditional guru. He was an outlaw. With the vegetarians he would eat meat, with the meat-eaters he would only eat vegetables. Whatever you had very neatly encapsulated as what the guru should be, he was not. Finally, you had to ask, "Well, who is he?" He is this huge, uncontrollable force. To meet this force in the form of a human being is to meet yourself.

Once I asked Papaji, "How is it possible that I can thank you for what you have given me?" Clearly he did not want anything. He was in his eighties. He led a very simple life. His children were married, and he didn't have an ashram to support, so I really didn't know how to express my thanks to him. He saw that it was a true question and he took it very seriously. He said, "Well, I will tell you. You give your whole life to This. Everything. You make *This* all."

When he said that, I knew it was profound, and I said, "Yes." If he hadn't said exactly that, who knows what would have happened? I might have started seeking again for another bigger, better experience. But to actually be invited to give my life to the Grace that appeared in it, not knowing where it would take me, was irresistible.

chapter thirteen

I'D BEEN IN HARDWAR a couple of weeks when Papaji invited me to his house. He was full of excitement and exclaimed, "Oh, I dreamed of you last night as the Goddess Ganga! Your name will be Ma Gangaji." I was delighted he had dreamed of me as Ganga because I knew how he treasured the Ganga River, but the thought came, "Oh, no. Does this mean I have to go back to the States with a Hindu name?" I could have sworn I would never be one of those people who had a Hindu name.

When I asked him what Gangaji means he said, "Anyone who is willing to bathe in the Ganga will be free. You will speak to people, and as you do, invite them *in*, so they can taste the freedom of the Ganga." He told me "ji" was added as a term of respect, so that people would see me as someone to pay attention to.

Soon after, I got sick with a very high fever, probably malaria. Papaji told me not to take any medicine right away. He said, "We have very good medicine here that will stop the fever, but let it go a few more nights and it will burn something. It can take care of some necessary business." In the delirium I felt I experienced the big bang. Many lifetimes flashed through. I knew myself as a cockroach; I knew myself as a powerful yogi. It was a huge event.

When I told Papaji about the phenomenal experiences I'd had, what he said surprised me. He advised me to take the medicine to bring down my temperature, and when my fever was gone to see what remained. I saw he was directing me to what is deeper than any experience. He wanted me to recognize what is untouched by the visionary state and the ordinary state, by suffering and bliss. When he saw that I saw, he was very happy.

Papaji formally asked me to go back to the West and share his message. When he did that I assured him it was a big mistake, that I was not ready for it. I thought, "What in the world does he mean? I am very comfortable as a student. I am a very practiced student. I know how to be a good student. But he is asking me to sit on a couch and be the teacher. I know nothing about that." I told him, "I know nothing about teaching this. I know nothing about Advaita Vedanta. I haven't even read Ramana's books, and you are asking me?"

He answered, "Just right. Just right. Only speak from your direct experience. Simply speak from your realization."

I could see that what he was asking me to do had nothing to do with mind. Initially it brought up fear and doubt, but they didn't have any substance; I couldn't follow them. I saw that Papaji knows what he says. So then if he's saying it, do I trust the fear and the doubt, or do I trust what he's saying? Do I trust my limitations and the certainty that I am limited, or do I trust Papaji?

Everything he had said to me up to that point had been proven by my experience. Why not listen to him? So I said, "All right." He told me, "Don't worry. You will have help."

He was right. It is absolutely true at every level. In satsang I don't know what I am going to say when I open my mouth. Sometimes it is only later, in reflection, that I get what was said. Sometimes I have to ask whoever is driving me home, "What was said then?" And I am not speaking about channeling other entities. I'm speaking about trusting the space of silence, about telling the truth, and about asking for help—always asking for help, always bowing to the help that is always present. This help is available for everyone. I don't receive it because I am some rare being. As you have seen, I am just like you. I would be happy to tell you if I weren't, but I am. So any help that is available to me is available to all.

I had asked for final help, and when I met Papaji I received final help. Then he really finalized it when he asked me to share his message. In doing that, he gave me a life that would allow no latitude. I said, "Use me," and he said, "All right. You now have a life where you have to speak the truth, live the truth. A life in which there is no room for the lie."

chapter fourteen

ON THAT FIRST visit to India I was the teacher's pet.
Papaji was treating me like I was very special, and everybody could see it. The friend I'd come to Lucknow with
hated me for it. Papaji had favored her first, because she
had an awakening. Then I had an awakening and he
turned all his energy toward me. When he asked me to
hold satsang she was the first one I wanted to tell. Eli was
there when Papaji asked me, so he already knew. I went
to my dear sister to share the good news. She just turned
on me. She said, "Humph. That couldn't be."

When I perceived her anger I felt that I had been

betrayed. I didn't understand. After all, we loved each other, and we had found Papaji together. The next time I saw Papaji I asked him, "How is it possible that somebody who knows me and loves me is not overflowing in joy with what is occurring?" His blunt reply was, "It is to be expected."

A year or two later my friend came to me and said that when I told her, she was jealous. It was subconscious to her at the time. When we talked we worked through it, which is why I can talk about it now.

When she responded the way she did, what came up for me was, "Oh, well, since she knows me, I guess she's right, so it couldn't be." But instead of attending to that I listened to Papaji and the power of his words. He had said, "It is to be expected." So my decision was, "Now, what will I be true to? Where is my attention? Is my attention on what someone is saying about me?" I saw how strong the tendency was to want her to see how wonderful this is, and how happy she could be too, and to want her to support me in it. But following those desires would take my attention away from true peace, and I listened to Papaji instead.

Papaji was right. Since I've been playing the role of teacher I've seen the same phenomenon happen around me. Whoever has been perceived to be close to me, beginning with Eli, has been an object of jealousy by others. When it was quite clear Eli was going to stay close to me, it became, "Okay, who is next closest to her?" Then that person became the focus of the projection "That one is in my way."

As for Eli, he tells the story of how absolutely perfect it was for him that I was asked to teach. In his initial visit with Papaji, Eli had realized the spiritual pride and arrogance that he had to face. In the moment when Papaji told him that he had plans for Eli beyond his wildest dreams and Eli knew he was being asked to teach, he cried and told Papaji that it was his wife who was the Satguru (the true teacher).

Eli is a man. He's a head man. He *is* a teacher. He got pushed deeper into the fire of whatever pride there was, so he got to burn a lot. He wasn't fighting the burning. As stuff came up he welcomed it. He loved it. He could always see the perfection of it. It was a push for me to let myself be out there and be seen as teacher. It was the

reverse for Eli to *not* be the teacher. So Papaji just flipped us both.

Essentially, what changed when I met Papaji was that where there had been conflict, there is peace. But outer things changed too. For instance, I haven't danced since that time, except at home. That was a big life-style change. When I stopped frantically dancing every chance I got, I had to start doing things like walking and swimming.

There was a period right after meeting Papaji when all my body disciplines fell away, but it didn't last. I even stopped doing yoga, which I had done regularly over many years. I gained thirty pounds and started getting very sick.

Part of the cultural milieu around Papaji was a denial of the body: "The body is nothing. Don't pay any attention to it." I bought that for a while. Then I recognized that is not the teaching, that is just part of his culture. I asked myself, "What is the teaching?" I saw it is fine to take care of the body. It is fine to take care of the earth. It is fine to take care of your house, your children, your pets.

Making the distinction between what is cultural and what is true was a growing point for me. The body disciplines came back but in an entirely different way. It wasn't because this body was going to give me something. It wasn't because the body was the ultimate vehicle of pleasure, or because I equated physical health with freedom. It wasn't that at all. No, the body is the body, and if there is unnecessary suffering in it, then let's take care of it.

One time when I was speaking to Papaji, he congratulated me. I thought he must have noticed how hard I had worked to get to where I was. Very quickly he caught me with his tiger's gaze and said, "Nothing you have done in this lifetime gave rise to this that you are being congratulated for." He pulled the rug out from under me and gave me the chance to float in the sea of natural humility. I thought, "*Nothing* I have done, and yet I am here. Grace beyond measure. Luck beyond deservability. That is what he is congratulating me for."

Another time Papaji saw me in a certain state and said, "There! That! Now, speak to me about it." I was experiencing myself as not human—as not anything. I said, "I can't," and he said, "Okay." A little later he again said, "Okay, right there! What are you experiencing? Now speak!" Finally I got irritated, thinking, "Why won't he leave me alone? Just leave me in samadhi." So I told him, "Papaji, I can't speak it. The truth can't be spoken. It is impossible to speak it and be in it." He replied, "Then come out of it and speak."

It was so perfect. That state of transcendence was actually bondage, the golden bondage. He slapped me out of nothingness into somethingness—stomach, heart, lungs, body, age, aches, sensation. It's clear to me that when Papaji asked me to speak he doomed me to failure. The truth cannot be spoken, and nevertheless, it must be spoken. It *must* be spoken. Sometimes it seems I come close, but I cannot say that I have ever really said what it is I must say.

In Lucknow on a later visit an interviewer gave Papaji a list of questions. Papaji asked a small group of us to answer them before the satsang. One of the questions was from someone who lived above an auto-body shop with very loud noise going twenty-four hours a day. He was wondering how he could keep his meditative practice, how he could keep his vigilance on what is still, in the face of his environment. Papaji asked each one of us what we would say. I remember my answer because I was very proud of it. I said, "Well, he just needs to find out what is unaffected by the noise, what is by its nature still."

The day of the interview came and we were all waiting to see how Papaji would answer these questions he had given us. When this particular question came up the man said, "I live over an auto-body shop and it is so noisy. How do I maintain my vigilance?" Papaji looked at him and said, "Move. Move to another place. What is the question here?" I saw how I had taken the teaching I received from him into my mind and used it to make a formula, even though there is no formula.

When it was drawing near to the end of my first six-week visit I went into a panic at the idea of leaving him—of leaving the immense love I felt for him. The panic was, "Oh my God, if I leave him, I leave this Grace, this Beauty, this Perfection, this obvious Truth of who I am."

I broke the rule, rushed over to his house and knocked on his door. Still at the doorway, I told him, "Papaji, I cannot go. I can't go back. I have to stay here with you." He nodded and invited me in and made some tea for us.

One of the things Papaji always loved was reading train schedules. "Well, let's see," he said. "The Lucknow Mail leaves at nine-thirty. That would get you to Delhi at a certain time. That will give you a couple of hours to get to the airport and take your plane. Then you have somebody meeting you in Hawaii when you get there."

I said, "No Papaji, you don't understand. I cannot leave. I cannot go." He looked at me very directly and said, "You have to go, so that you can see what does not go."

GANGAJI

chapter fifteen

ELI AND I returned to Maui and stayed in a simple motel on the beach because we had sublet our house. I missed Papaji incredibly. I missed the spaciousness and grace that surrounded him. I was in Maui, but it was so American. All its charms had disappeared.

At night I would be torn apart with longing and misery, and my mind got very active. There was a turmoil inside me with all my self-doubt saying, "I shouldn't have left Papaji. I should still be there. Oh, I should never have even met Papaji if this is the result. I made a huge mistake. Now what good are all of the realizations I had with him? I have never been more miserable."

It was four in the morning and I was in my bed, unable to sleep. I felt like I was being tossed against the walls of the room. And then, by grace, a moment of true inquiry appeared. "Tell the truth. What is happening, really, right now?" I acknowledged, "I'm not with him. That's the way it is. All of this discussion is absurd." Enormous fear and anguish arose in the form of, "Well, what will I do? What does it mean? What is going to happen?" And then I remembered what he had said to me. He had said, "Stop! Stop where you are. Give up your techniques, your strategies. Give up your story. Just stop."

In a crystal instant, I stopped. I stopped fighting the longing. I stopped trying to figure out what it was I should do to escape the misery. I stopped trying to get to sleep. In that moment I recognized there is no guru sitting some place other than where I am. He, Papaji, is my own Self.

I recognized all of life as the truth of who I am, not just this particular life stream. I saw the turmoil as a kind of internal, subconscious resistance to the teaching. I was making the teaching be about *him* and about it looking a certain way, with me physically at his side. But suddenly there was perfect clarity. There was no absence, whatsoever. No separation, whatsoever.

I have always been profoundly thankful for that dark night of the soul. It got my attention in a way that all the bliss and happiness, and all the closeness to Papaji couldn't. When I was with him I was just too happy, and it was absolutely necessary for me to meet my demons.

Soon afterward we went to California so Eli could teach at Esalen. I would say that's where the major, the essential shift occurred. It was the end of May and we were having a quiet evening in our room. It must have been a Wednesday, because on Wednesdays the people working there got the evening off. Suddenly, and very simply, I realized the whole structure that supported my story was gone. All the scaffolding was gone. Every single thing that held it together—gone. It was as if a thunderbolt split open my mind and annihilated any possibility of lasting doubt about what is real. There was the clearest and most precise recognition that it is all Oneself. But *really, truly.* I started laughing out loud, laughing and laughing.

Eli immediately understood and wrote to Papaji about it. I called Papaji the next day, but I couldn't communicate it on the phone because of the bad connection and his deafness. What I was laughing about can't be put into words, but it had to do with how much physical, mental and emotional energy was wrapped up in "me." In "me" getting something, in "me" getting rid of something, in "me" getting enlightened, in "me" finding happiness, getting eternal health, or eternal youth, or riches. In me, me, me. That struck me as being so funny! It was such a great joke that I couldn't stop laughing. Since then it is not that this "me," this Gangaji person, is excluded. But there is energy, energy overflowing, available for my Self, which is the totality of Being.

At breakfast the following morning a woman in Eli's group was sitting beside me in the dining hall. She began shaking. She said, "I feel something very intense, some burning. I don't know what's happening! Do you know what's happening?" She felt there was something coming from me to her.

I told her Papaji had told me that I would be teaching and if she had any questions I'd be happy to talk to her. Since Eli had been speaking about Papaji in the group, she already knew something about him. I suggested she come up to our room later. Then, maybe five people began coming over after Eli's sessions. That's how the teaching started to happen.

AT ESALEN

I'd had this overwhelming, indescribable realization of
the ground of true fulfillment and happiness, regardless of
the insanity of my mind, my emotions, my past, or my
nervous system. I felt that I had to share it with my
brother, sister and father. I wrote my father a letter, sending him a picture of Papaji, saying, "Look! See how you
and Papaji look alike!" But he didn't see it. My sister sent
me several Christian tracts about how low self-esteem

could be resolved in surrender to Christ. My brother said, "Well, you know, Toni was always a little crazy." So what to do? What to do?

The truth is, not everyone is interested in realization, and you can't force that interest. I don't know if the interest is a result of maturity, or if it is grace, or if it just occurs randomly. Unless someone is genuinely interested in the issues of reality and finality, speaking of realization simply doesn't make sense.

I used to send my father information published by the Gangaji Foundation, and when I would talk to him he'd say, "Well, Honey, I read what you sent me, but I didn't understand a word." In the mid-nineties, as he was starting to decline, I went to visit him. That's when I just gave up. I gave up trying to get him to see what I had seen. Nothing I said meant anything to him. He simply was not interested.

On that visit I began to watch football with him because that was what he liked to do. It was a way for us to be together. From the time I was a teenager I had hated watching football. When a game came on TV I would leave the room in disgust, but now I was willing. One day we were watching a game. Unexpectedly, he turned to me and said, "Why, Toni, I believe you're happy." That's really what parents want for their children, for them to be happy. I said, "Yes, Daddy, I am." And that was it. In seeing that he was freed from the bondage that often exists in the parent-child relationship. Although he had never been able to give me the secret that unlocked the storehouse of happiness, he could see it was unlocked. We sat watching Ole Miss play football on TV—happy parent,

happy child. So he too benefited from my meeting Papaji.

In Lucknow it had been quite funny and wonderful when I learned that Papaji was crazy about the game of cricket. I'd found myself watching cricket matches on TV with him, the very thing that I'd spent so much energy trying to escape from with my father. So I had to see the issue wasn't real. My whole rebellion against my father's lifestyle was just me trying to escape my own unhappiness. It had nothing to do with anything else. How perfect the universe is, right up in your face.

chapter sixteen

ELI AND I returned to India to see Papaji again in September of the same year we met. I was in a great hurry to get back to him, but when he saw me he said, "What are you doing back here so soon?" On the first visit he had been only confirming and inviting. Now he was testing and pushing. He definitely wasn't treating me like his special pet anymore. Right away my personal patterns of identification came up.

I began to tell a familiar story about not being appreciated, or not being seen. "Why doesn't he love me?" I could feel it and hear it begin in my mind. By grace, I realized, "Don't do this. Don't follow that story here." I had followed that with my parents and lovers and husbands, and I knew how foolish it would be to treat Papaji the way I treated everyone else in my life.

During the next visits there were many occasions to see, "Well, this is not the way it was with him before," or, "This is not what I expected," followed by the opportunity to see, "What do I make of this?" There was no question about the decision not to make of it what I had made of all the other events in my life.

One day at Papaji's house in Lucknow there were a lot

of people in the living room. A little hallway led to the kitchen. He was in there and I was with him with a smaller group. There was the feeling, "Oh, we are the privileged ones in here with him." He looked at me and he just scowled. He said, "What are you doing here? Go out there and be with the people."

In that moment I saw I was really trying to keep something for myself. To that degree, even though I was in extreme bliss at the time, I was suffering. Suffering, even in bliss! When I let go of that it no longer mattered about being up close to him. I opened my heart to see him everywhere. It was such a beautiful teaching. He sent me away from him to be with all. In being with all, I find him.

I remember marveling at how he made use of normal human attributes in the people around him. At the time I had just started to have meetings with people, and a man from Maui was also having meetings. Papaji turned to me and said, "Aha, Gangaji, I hear this man is having lots more people than you are. Is that true?"

A sense of competition rose up, and then, within a blink, I felt shame for feeling it. When I looked at Papaji I saw he was playing with me. When he was teasing you his eyes would have a certain glint and there was a particular set to his mouth. I laughed. I realized that characteristics like ambition, which are part of the cellular, genetic, or conditioned makeup, are no problem when they are truly in service to the truth of who you are.

Papaji was unrestrained in fanning the flames of our desire for freedom. He wanted people to know its value, and that you have to be willing to give your whole life for it.

He told us an amazing story about meeting a yogi on the road in the forest. This yogi had wondrous powers that his master had passed on to him, but he didn't have the power of freedom. His master had told him he would have to meet someone else who could give him that power, because he himself hadn't realized freedom.

When the yogi and Papaji met they recognized one another. He recognized that Papaji had something to teach him that he was looking for, and Papaji recognized him as someone who was actually open to receiving what he had to give. The two of them sat by a campfire in the hills above Rishikesh and talked.

Over the course of the night the man was able to tell Papaji all the different things he had mastered. He could move his body from one place to another through the etheric realms. He could read minds. He had the power of controlling his physiological functions. And he had the most treasured power of all: the power of immortality of the body. It was held in his walking staff that was always with him.

Papaji reminded him, "But there is one thing you don't have," and the man replied, "Yes, that's true. My teacher was not able to transmit freedom to me. I see in your eyes that you have it and that you have the power to transmit it. Will you transmit it to me?"

Papaji asked, "What will you give for it?" The yogi answered, "Everything. I will give you anything for that power, because while all of these powers I have are amazing, the power of freedom is the sweetest, and it eludes me."

Papaji saw that the yogi was sincere. He reached over and took the man's staff of immortality and broke it over his knee and threw it into the fire. He said, "Now you will live and die as other men. This body that you have is no longer special. The remarkable power that you had was able to be disposed of. Now you have the capacity to discover what is true. Now you will recognize your eternal Self."

Papaji purposely introduced Eli and me to his own master, Sri Ramana Maharshi, right before we were leaving from our second visit to India. We knew something big was happening because he gave us both pictures of Ramana he'd cut out from a magazine to take with us on the trip home.

That same night we were in our hotel room in Delhi. Looking into those pictures, feeling Ramana's aliveness, there was an authentic visitation from Sri Ramana. It was so real. I could say it was psychedelic, but that trivializes it. I don't know how to talk about it. I recognized Ramana as Stillness *conscious of itself*—perfect, clear, pristine, awake, formless intelligence.

Papaji often talked about his teacher at his satsangs. As a guru, he said, Ramana offered no special powers. He pointed only to the freedom inherent in pure consciousness recognizing Itself. Once I asked Papaji what "Ramana" meant and he told me, "That which abides in the heart of all being."

When he was a sixteen-year-old boy Ramana had a strong premonition of death. Instead of trying to escape

SRI RAMANA MAHARSHI

the ancient, primordial fear, instead of seeking some distraction or running for help, he simply lay down on the floor and experienced the fear totally. As he lay perfectly still his body went into rigor mortis. Not knowing if it would be the end of his young life, he followed the profound command to meet death all the way. In that, he discovered what is untouched by the death of form.

I had first seen a picture of Ramana back when Eli and I were going to Berkeley for our t'ai chi classes and I was getting interested in acupuncture. In the afternoon we would often have time to go to Shambhala Books on Telegraph Avenue where there was a huge photograph of him on the wall. He was beautiful, and I could feel his radiance, but what I saw was a gentle, removed saint who didn't have much relevance to me and my desires. At that time what was more important to me than his countenance was that he had horrible posture. Overlooking the gift of liberation in the search for physical perfection, my judgment had been, "I wouldn't want to follow him because I wouldn't want to end up looking like that."

While Papaji was a man in the world with jobs, a house, possessions, and children to marry off, his teacher had been a hermit. Ramana only had a loin cloth, a couch to lie on, and a mountain to walk around. His invitation—to experience death before your body dies—has nothing to do with what you do in the world.

People came to Ramana and said, "I will never get enlightened because I have too many duties in the world. I need to drop all that and come be a sadhu." Ramana replied, "If you were meant to be a sadhu, you would be a sadhu."

Papaji told a revealing story about himself. After he had been with Ramana for four or five years, Ramana called Papaji to him. This was shortly after the war for independence, when India had been partitioned. He said, "Look at what is happening in India. It is a mess, and your family is in the Punjab. They are Hindus living in Muslim territory and in great danger, so they need to get out. Go get them out."

Papaji answered, "But Bhagavan, none of that exists. It is all a dream. You are all that exists. The Grace of you is my only reality, and so being here with you is the only thing that is important or real."

Ramana looked at him for a second and said, "Yes, yes, and since it is a dream, what is the problem? Go get your people out of the Punjab."

Papaji did what his guru told him. He left Ramana and never sat with him physically again. At great personal risk he rescued a hundred of his relatives and got them established in Lucknow. Then he became part of the work force for a number of years, having satsang quietly on the side until after his children were married.

It is such a great teaching. Ramana was naturally a sadhu, living a sadhu's life, having no concern with anything except the truth of the absolute, eternal presence of Self. If people came to hear him, they came to hear him. If they fed him, he was fed. If they didn't, he didn't eat. It didn't matter. Because of the tendency of the mind to search for models, it is easy to look at Ramana and say, "Aha, that is what it is to live in truth." But there is no particular way that living in truth looks.

In my first visits Papaji and I had very intense conversations. He would question and push me. He didn't let me escape from whatever it was I thought was obstructing me from Truth. Then, after my second visit, my questions were finished and we no longer engaged in that way. It got so that the only words that passed between us were words like "pass the sugar" or "close the door." After a certain point of hearing, a certain point of receiving, the communion between us was inexpressible in words.

For the first few years after we left India I was writing

Papaji often, sometimes three letters a day. The letters were outpourings of my gratitude and realization, my adoration of him and what he had shown me. This writing, writing, writing must have lasted three or four years. Over time the rhythm of the writing changed. I was not writing every day, and then I would maybe go for a couple of months without writing. Then I'd write him every day for a week or two.

I always loved getting a letter from him, but I never expected him to write back. He had given me so much. Right away, early, I said, "You've given me everything. I just want the rest of this life to be an expression of that." So that's what the letters were, and they just had to be written. I couldn't *not* write them, nor could I force them.

chapter seventeen

PAPAJI WAS ALWAYS unpredictable, uncontrollable and undeniable. Soon after we met he wanted me to give satsang in some of the holy places of India. I felt resistance, but he was very determined, requesting it repeatedly over a couple of years. It was a complicated trip to arrange logistically, in part because it was so difficult to find clean food and housing. For a while I thought maybe I wouldn't have to do it, but Papaji kept pushing the project. He personally got other people involved and arranged for them to go with me.

Bodh Gaya, the place where the Buddha woke up, was especially primitive, but Papaji insisted I give satsang there. When I went, in the summer of 1994, ten thousand Tibetan Buddhists were camping in the town. Walking to satsang I had to pick my way through human excrement. I got sick, extremely sick, and was barely able to get around.

The trip was so horrible—beautiful and horrible. I didn't ever want to do it again. Afterward I told Papaji I felt Bodh Gaya wasn't really the right place for me, that it was too Buddhist. Do you know what he said to me then?

ON THE GANGA AT VARANASI

He said, "Yes, I always wondered why you wanted to go to Bodh Gaya."

I visited Papaji five times from 1990 until 1995. Every visit was filled with grace and deeper discovery. Then it was clear that those trips to India were over. The last time I was with him I knew that it was the last time I'd be with him in form. I didn't know what would happen. I suspected maybe he would die. I knew the preciousness of being with him. It was incredibly sweet. Then, somehow, that was it. I wouldn't be traveling back to India to see him again. There was never any conflict. There was never anything from his side like, "Why aren't you here?" It was very clear between us by then.

Papaji had no problem teaching me from afar. In satsang a man spoke to me about his mantra. Very conscientiously, I told him there is nothing wrong with a mantra. A mantra can be helpful. It can be beautiful, but it is not really what this teaching from Ramana and Papaji is about. This teaching has nothing to do with any spiritual practice. This teaching is about what exists before the mantra, during the mantra, and after the mantra.

The next day, *the next day*, I got a letter from a friend who was happy to share with me the mantra that Papaji had just given her! That was so good. I saw that there's a time to take on mantra and a time to give up mantra. Again I was being shown there is no place to hold onto, no ledge that is solid to stand on. Papaji called it "non-abidance in the mind *anywhere*." That's the real invitation from Papaji, and the acceptance of it is the acceptance of seeing how the mind busily constructs the next ledge.

Sometimes Papaji would say something that I only understood later. One of his most profound statements was, "Wait and see." At first I just dismissed it, assuming I knew what he meant. He would say it a lot. "Wait and see. Wait and see." And then one day, when I was back home, I heard it. "Oh, wait and see."

We are so used to having to know what our lives will be like. We feel we need that image for our safety, or so we can do it right, or so we won't make a mistake. But what Papaji was saying was, "No. Experience what is here. Just be who you are in this not-knowingness." The more deeply "wait and see" is heard, the more profound the revelation.

After the first satsangs in Eli's and my room at Esalen, the meetings grew and grew. The next time we went back to Esalen there were maybe fifteen people, so we moved into the dining room. Then there were forty people. Also, I was traveling with Eli to Europe and there were lots of people coming there, maybe a hundred.

On the first trip to Europe I began to feel some kind of self-importance, some, "Oh, I am the guru. I am the teacher." Seeing myself as a guru was a trap, but Papaji was so present in me by that point that it was as if I could feel a kind of mental slap from him. "Who do you think you are? You're nothing."

The mind has a tendency to own whatever is happening and say, "I did it." Pretty soon just hearing "I did it" *is* the admonition of the guru. Right along with the thought, in the moment of thinking it, is the correction.

It's so clear that giving satsang has nothing to do with me. Satsang makes use of my personality, my experiences, and my intellect, or my lack of intellect, my humor, my voice, or whatever, but it has nothing to do with all of that. If someone sees me as guru that simply means they are using me in some mysterious way to reveal what is true, to reveal what is alive, what is free, what holds both guru and disciple, both teacher and student.

There were people in the States who thought it was very inappropriate for me to speak. Many had meditated a lot longer than I had, and maybe had bigger and higher experiences. Who did I think I was? And of course, that was appropriate. They had to challenge me. Who am I to say "I am pure radiant consciousness"? What do I mean by that? It rattled a lot of people when this western woman, just like other western women, came back from India saying this.

I remember a friend who knew me as Toni came to an early satsang and left before it was over. After the meeting I asked what happened to her. On her way out she told someone, "Oh, I came to see Gangaji, but when I saw Gangaji was only Toni, I decided to leave."

chapter eighteen

I KNOW THAT TO some people I have been, and am, an object of devotion. When devotion is pure, when it's simply an out-bursting of the heart, it is beautiful. I know that from being with Papaji. Until I met him, when I was with teachers and groups I really tried to be in devotion, because I could see that those were the people who were getting it. I tried, but pretty soon that would become tiresome because there was some effort involved.

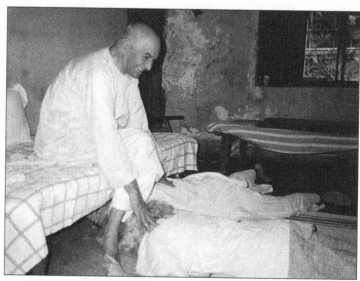

ELI AND I AT PAPAJI'S FEET

Every opportunity I had with Papaji in India my legs would just fall out from under me, and I was prostrate at his feet. There is a huge "Thank you, I love you" that arises, a bowing that takes place in the heart toward that one who reveals your true nature. Of course, in this culture, physical bowing doesn't fit, but when the devotion is clean, however it's expressed, it's beautiful. If it's not clean, it is sickening.

I'm just like anybody. It feels good to me to be loved and appreciated. It's certainly more enjoyable than being hated and disrespected. But, though I know I'm loved, I'm not under any illusion that it is me that is responsible for the love. The devotion is there because of what this human form is used for, what it reveals in the person who is loving. Really, it is not personal. The personal may be included, but it's not personal.

There are people who see me as their sister, or the Anti-Christ, or the enemy. Some see me as supremely interesting. To others I am superficial and boring. Some people see me as a teacher passing through with something precious to offer. Others see me as a charlatan, part of the "great guru scam." But all of that's irrelevant, because it has nothing to do with who I really am.

At the first satsang at the farm where we lived in Maui, I just said what came. Before the second satsang I thought, "There are certain points I want everyone to see: permanence and impermanence, grasping and rejecting. Those are the points I have to cover." So I wrote them down carefully on a piece of paper, and then I delivered them. People just looked at me. I wadded up my piece of paper and threw it away. It was obvious the people who came to see me knew all the information. They knew too much information. What was required was not that I pass along more or better information. No, it was that I stop, that I stop passing information, that I stop everything and just be still. In that, it is possible to see what has never been seen and attempt to speak that.

The same year that I met Papaji, 1990, a well-known Indian guru named Osho died. That's when a lot of westerners who had been students of Osho discovered Papaji, so they also discovered Gangaji. They started coming to satsang at the farm. One day so many people came to satsang that I really thought the living room floor was going to crash. We had to build a platform down on the lower

SATSANG IN MAUI

part of the land. When there were too many people for the platform we moved the meetings to a Waldorf School. I think there were two or three hundred people then. Many of them were very lively and energetic and excited to find a new teaching, since their teacher had died.

Eli totally supported satsang. He provided whatever I wanted or needed, and he was also being my student. His job wasn't always easy because the people in Maui had a tradition of coming late for everything. I wanted the satsangs to be respected and not treated like just another Maui happening, so I asked Eli to stand at the door and not let people who arrived late come in until after the meditation was over. He met a lot of resistance, but he was willing to do it.

The last time we had satsang at the farm the house was packed. I had just received a letter from Papaji. I was thinking he was somewhere in India and I was waiting to get back to see him. I walked into the room to speak. When I looked out at the faces of the people I was talking to, I saw Papaji's face in *everyone*. Not the features, but his *face*. What a mystery!

When we got back from our first trip to India I wrote to the teacher I'd learned about Papaji from, sharing the great joy of meeting Papaji. Soon after, he and Papaji had a falling-out. Papaji said his former student was not teaching what he had received from Papaji. Papaji asked me to meet with the people in the Bay Area who had left that teacher, and with the ones that teacher had kicked out, in order to bring them Papaji's message.

First I met with some of Papaji's supporters in the area

to be sure that they supported me, and they did. Then I began meeting privately with individuals and having small meetings in Oakland. Once, Papaji's former student showed up at a small satsang and we had a real confrontation. We wrote each other a couple of letters after that, but we weren't truly connecting with each other. Finally, I had to let it go.

Satsang in the Bay Area grew. A woman who had been sitting with Papaji's ex-disciple was at the meeting in Oakland he had come to, and she invited me to give satsang in Boulder. At Papaji's request, a couple from Boulder who'd met him in Lucknow joined with her to invite me. That was the first place I went that had no connection with Eli's groups. We didn't know if anybody would show up.

When I got to Boulder I was given one of those magazines that shows what all the people in the counterculture are doing in town. I read, "This spiritual teacher will give you powers that you never had." "With this one you will have wonderful sex for the rest of your life." "With this one you will never grow old." "This one will get you enlightened in three sessions." I thought, "What am I doing in this place? What do they want from me?"

I realized, "Well, I have no idea what they want. I will just go, and I will bring them Papaji's invitation, which is to discover the truth of who one is." No power, no great sex, no immortal life of the body, no quick fixes, just the truth of who one is. I was astounded at the hunger for that simplicity, and the "Yes" in the acceptance of that invitation.

I had no idea, I *have* no idea, of what is wanted. All I can do, as a person, is be true to what I have experienced, and express it the best I can. Whether that is a good expression, or a great expression, or a poor expression, or the same as every other expression is really not my business. If I make that my business then my attention is diverted from the Truth that must be expressed.

When I was in Boulder some people from Santa Fe invited me to come there. I started keeping a schedule where I would stay a month at a place. I would come to the Bay Area for a month. Then I would go to Boulder for a month, Santa Fe for a month, then India, then back to Hawaii. I was traveling all the time.

It became clear that living in Maui and doing all the traveling we were doing was just too hard. Some people asked me to move to Boulder. I stayed there for a few months in a little house that was rented for me. I definitely considered, "Do I move to Boulder?" or, "Do Eli and I move to Boulder?" But I didn't like the altitude and besides, we liked the Bay Area. It is more our style. So that's where we moved.

Packing for the move from Maui back to California I looked at some of my old journals, written between 1975 and when we went to India in 1990. Those reflections were definitely neurotic, but there was a strand of truth throughout. It was as if the truth had been pushing my neuroses up in my face so they could be seen. I could make out how my neuroses had defined me in some way—some kind of dramatic, suffering, *special* way—and defining myself as "special" wasn't special at all. In fact, in the South we use the expression, "It's common as dirt." I saw that all my attempts to define myself as special were just that common.

When I first met Papaji he told me, "You are the one. You are the one I have been waiting for." I thought, "Finally I am seen, I am the one! I am the *One!*" Several days later some new people came to his house. I was there when he greeted everyone and told them, "You are the one I have been waiting for." It was very good because I got to see, "Yes, it is the same One. I am not so special. Everyone is the same One." The willingness to give up specialness was required for what has been here all along to claim Itself.

In the beginning of my giving satsang Eli drove me around and cooked for me and sort of took care of me, but then he needed to return to work. He was still teaching a few groups but not nearly as many as before. He had dropped almost everything to focus on me, support my satsang, and to publish *Wake Up and Roar*, the first book he compiled of Papaji's edited talks. We had run through the money we made on the sale of the Mill Valley house and he needed to generate some income.

The organization around me at that time was incredibly loose. Donations were accepted to pay for expenses, and sometimes I'd be given a wad of money, literally fistfuls of dollars, depending on how much was collected and the expense of the hall. Somebody had the presence of mind to say, "Wait a minute, we need some structuring. We need to set up a foundation." So in 1993 the Gangaji

Foundation was formed in Boulder. Once that was in place and there were some volunteers to help take care of me, Eli became less involved.

From the beginning the Foundation wasn't collecting enough money at the events to cover the costs. Even though some people would come to satsang without donating, there were always some generous ones who covered the expenses at the last minute, but it was taxing for those putting it on. Almost every month someone would ask, "Please, can we charge money?" and I'd say, "We can't."

At some point I had a good conversation with a friend who's a spiritual teacher. That's when I got clear about the issue in my own mind. In the East they don't have to charge because the devotees give their teachers everything, but this is a different culture. It turned out that what we were doing was worse than charging. We were begging people for money at the end of each satsang. So I said, "Okay, we won't charge, but we'll ask for a suggested donation at the door."

Then I asked myself what Papaji would think. Papaji never charged for his satsangs. I wrote him and told him what was happening. He wrote back, saying, "Of course, it is fine." Even so, we never have turned anybody away for not paying. So the business end of it has been interesting: how to conduct business about something that is not a business.

The woman who originally invited me to Boulder became the first Director of the Gangaji Foundation. She really picked it up off the ground and made it into something. She was creative, strong, and very devoted to spreading Papaji's invitation. After she left, the Foundation continued to grow and evolve.

I'm not interested in having an ashram or a school. I love the work the Foundation does, and I love the arena that it gives people for working together. I've never known how long the Foundation was supposed to last. I still don't. It's been amazing to me how beautifully it's been supported. We don't have reservoirs of money, but we're not in debt, and it's always worked out.

chapter nineteen

I HAVE OFTEN SAID that the most important day in my life was the day I met my teacher. Then, in 1997, at the age of eighty-six, a ripe old age for an Indian, he died.

I have to say that day was also the most important day in my life. Those two together are the most important days—his appearance in my life and his disappearance from my life. For me, the form of Papaji didn't exist before 1990. Then it existed for seven years. His form hasn't existed since 1997. But what his form always pointed to was that which was here before he entered into my life, and what is here after he is gone from my life.

When Papaji died I was profoundly sad, totally sad, exquisitely sad, not keeping out sadness in the least. Not dissociated from deep grief, not being bigger than grief, not being so enlightened that there is no grief, just exquisitely, profoundly, deeply sad. That depth of sadness is bliss itself. I thought I had known grief before, but what I knew was some dramatization of grief. I didn't know the fullness of grief because I had tried to keep it away, and so I had only seen its back side.

I am happy to tell the world, "Yes, I am profoundly
sad at this loss of Papaji's form." Because this is *life*, not
some version of life. It's not some story of life. It's *life*.
Everything is included here. In the midst of sadness, I am

exquisitely joyful at the realization that what Papaji *is* can never be lost, what Papaji *is* has not shifted one iota with the dissolution of his form. In his disappearance I was forced to see that who he *is*, *really*, cannot disappear; that who he is, *really*, is who I am, and I am here.

You know, in everyone's life, everyone else will disappear sooner or later. Who knows who goes first? Sooner or later, everyone disappears. That is the ruthlessness and the beauty of our experience on earth. Only in realizing the truth of death can we fully experience life's preciousness.

Someone asked me recently what had been the biggest change in my life in the last several years. When I investigated, I realized I am more ordinary than I ever was before. The extraordinary event in this life was that I met Papaji. Until then I looked everywhere for the transcendental or the extraordinary, but after meeting Papaji I began to find the extraordinary in every moment. The mystery reveals itself in each everyday moment.

My daily life looks like any other life. It probably looks more boring than a lot of lives. I love to spend time with my husband. I like to go for walks and read books and go to the movies. I read two newspapers a day. Doing laundry is the only housework I enjoy, and ironing is one of my favorite things because I find it relaxing. I spend time shopping—not that I love to shop, but I do like good food and nice clothes and nice things. So you can see I don't live a saintly life. Everyone who knows me well knows I am not a saint.

But this ordinary life is filled with love. It is filled with peace. Moments of discomfort and unhappiness come, but those moments are always on an ocean of peace. The moments pass, but this ocean of love and peace doesn't go anywhere. I know it to be bottomless. Endless. Limitless. I know it to be who I am.

In Conversation

Dᴜʀɪɴɢ ᴛʜᴇ ᴍᴏɴᴛʜs *we met Gangaji and I talked things over that didn't fit neatly within the chronology of her story, but that filled out my understanding. The questions and answers in this section are drawn from those conversations.*

Rᴏslyn : *How is it that you agreed to work on this book?*

Gangaji: It was kind of a surprise to me. After I received your letter asking me to do it, first there was a "no" internally. Then a "Well, let's see." Then there was this really strong "Yes." In my mind I didn't think it was time for an autobiography, and I wasn't particularly interested in talking about these things. The thought that a book about me might actually be published is a little embarrassing. Plus, it doesn't even make sense. The supposed facts are so fluid.

When I am telling stories about myself, I don't even know if they're true. In fact, I know they're not true. The way I remember an event changes each time I tell it, because of the time that has elapsed since it was last told, and because of my shifting moods and changing hormones affect my memory of it.

That's all mental though. The "Oh my God, oh no! I'm going to talk about this?!" was coming from my mind. When I let that go it was "Why not?" The "yes" was deeper than the resistance, so the choice for me was just to surrender to it.

When you agreed, what came into my mind was that maybe you had no choice. Maybe because my prayer was a true prayer you had to answer it.

Oh [laughing heartily] I guess so. That's good. A true prayer is irresistible, so that catches us both.

Right. Because on some level, I am just as surprised to be doing this as you.

Yes, I know that about you, so it's a full yes then. I know that both of our intentions are that this be used for people to discover what's true, what's here. So that's what we want our time together to serve. Then who am I to say no? Better to say yes, and then let's see what happens.

❖ ❖ ❖ ❖ ❖

In "River of Freedom," the video documentary about you, Eli says that when he met you in 1975, your most striking feature was your commitment to Truth.

It wasn't truth with a capital "t" that Eli was talking about, though. When we first met, for me it was about

being honest, emotionally
honest. I didn't know about
Truth, per se, then. Eli was
really committed to truth
with a capital "T," and I was
committed to truth with a
small "t." That's one of the
things that made it such an
important meeting. Finally,
you can't have one without
the other, although there is
a tendency for people who
are committed to relative
truth to overlook absolute
truth, and vice versa.

In our relationship I kept bringing us back to the relative truth. "What's causing the suffering here, what's
really going on, what is this really about?" In my first
marriage I had a direct experience of the burden of the
lie, and after I gave up taking refuge in the lie, the truth
was very important to me. I believe that's what Eli was
referring to.

*I remember when I used to hear you talk about telling the
truth, about being true to the Truth, I thought you meant the relative truth, like what was going on in the moment. Then it seems
that what I was hearing changed to meaning telling the truth
about the absolute, about what's always here, regardless of what's
going on in the moment.*

Ahh, that's right. I think that's a natural progression. You start with relative truth because that's what you know, and that's what you've been lying about, so that's the beginning. That will lead you to the deeper truth. It's the same with mind and awareness. You start with investigating mind and that naturally leads you to awareness, because mind comes from awareness, just as relative truth comes from absolute truth.

What can be said about your relationship with Eli now?

As I've said, when our relationship began Eli was my teacher. Then that flipped. Now neither one of us sees the other as teacher or student. That's not what our relationship is based on. It's one Self, as husband and wife, as best friends.

How did that switch come about?

It happened incrementally. The teacher-student relationship was wearing for both of us. I think it was somehow necessary to Eli to go through that, and maybe for me too. After a while, living with your teacher can be like living with a cop, and I'm not interested in being someone's cop. So we just let those roles go.

Can I ask you about your sex life?

I've learned not to talk about Eli's and my sexual life publicly. It's private. Besides, I don't want anyone to fall into the trap of copying me, or using my experience as a justification for their behavior, or as an argument against their partner's. Each life unfolds uniquely.

There's such a strong charge around sex. Once, a few years ago, Eli and I spoke openly to an interviewer in Germany about our sexual relations. Afterward, people at our meetings there were very stirred up. They were arguing about whether or not Eli and I should be involved with sex after awakening. It became the pros against the cons! But that isn't the point. The point is sex stays or it goes, and it doesn't matter.

In the past you've occasionally joined Eli to teach with him at the events his foundation, the Leela Foundation, puts on. Now you've committed to work with him more often and more regularly.

When Eli and I first came together we were with each other twenty-four hours a day. That continued for many years. Then, after we met Papaji, we were apart for months at a time. Now it is quite clear it's time to spend more time together. I am drawn to that and so is he.

I don't have the physical steam to meet with as many groups as I did ten years ago. I am winding down, physically. That is just the fact of the matter. I feel good, I feel healthy, but when I'm traveling a lot, I don't feel good or healthy. Papaji, or the Hindu influence, would say, "So what? It doesn't matter." But paying attention to my body and taking care of it is the Taoist influence ingrained in me.

Working together is both a physical and a mysterious draw, and it's just time. Teaching with Eli is definitely different for me than teaching on my own. We both want to continue meeting groups individually, and now also together.

Gangaji, how is your daughter, Sarah?

She is doing very well. As an adult, Sarah lives a conventional life. I tell her she's living the life that I left, the one I jerked her out of, and she is very happy to be living it. Our relationship is wonderful.

She's a high-energy, intelligent woman and a good mother. She and her husband have four children and they are devoted to their family. She just had a new baby. They live in the Midwest and she comes with the kids to visit every year. I get to play grandma, which is really fun, precious, and sometimes exhausting. The oldest is only seven. She had so many of them so fast.

What does she think about you being a spiritual teacher?

When I got back from India the first time I think she was happy for me. Her attitude was, "Great, Mom's made guru." I don't know what she thinks about my role as spiritual teacher now. I really can't say what she sees. When we're together we're just being together, maybe speaking at a superficial level, but meeting at a much deeper level. We aren't talking satsang. She doesn't want me teaching her anything.

Do you have what people call a social life?

No. There are a couple of people that I occasionally take walks with and I love that, but Eli and I don't have a social life independent of our work and our families. I enjoy the social events that are connected with the Foundation.

How is it going with the Foundation at this point?

It is going beautifully. I am in awe of the wholehearted support I get from the Foundation staff and all the volunteers. With their help, this message is being heard all over the world.

Even now we rely on private donations to support

AT A VOLUNTEER PICNIC

most of our programs. Some of our donors got hurt badly in the stock market, so the turn in the economy has been challenging. It's always worked out, but it wouldn't without people's generosity.

I'm not that involved in the business end of the Foundation, and have never been involved in the day-to-day operation. I look at the business plan but allocating money is not something I have any talent for. I can barely manage my own household finances.

Once there was a Foundation we needed people on staff, so now there are salaried positions. It can get sticky though. One year I was feeling overly exhausted and needed to cancel some events. We saw it was necessary to downsize. So that was tricky, because then there were these beautiful people who were without a job. Life is messy.

What I really love is watching people rise to the occasion, grow and mature, and have their way of being in the world be true and clear and representative of this teaching. I'm very happy with the Foundation that way.

❖ ❖ ❖ ❖ ❖

Over the years, have your or other people's expectations of what a realized person should act like been a burden to you?

Not really. Pretty early, after returning from India, I recognized my tendency to try to imitate form. It's something I had been doing all my life, something everybody does. We model what is in front of us or what we think is better, and try to do that. When I first started speaking I had a habit of wearing leotards and a skirt. One day in satsang I looked up and all the women in the front row were wearing leotards and a skirt!

The tendency to imitate—in my case, what I thought the life of an awakened person should look like—was still the same old thing. So I stopped fighting my life as it is,

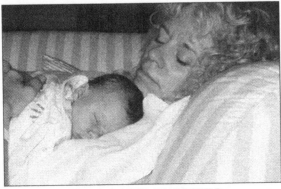

WITH MY FIRST GRANDCHILD

as this particular kind of person. In the early satsangs I felt it necessary to continually announce to people, "You have to be really clear that this is just your regular, bourgeois woman here. I am not a sadhu or a saint or an ascetic. In case you are looking for one, or expecting me to be one, I am not that."

Sometimes people still have artificial expectations of me. One time a woman hit my car with her car. Being hit upset me, and it didn't matter so much about the car. She and I began to talk and she said it was my fault. It wasn't my fault because I was driving down a street and she ran a stop sign and hit me. I said, somewhat heatedly, "It is not my fault, it is your fault!"

She paused, and looked at me. Then, as if she had nailed me, she said, "Hah! I know who you are. You are Gangaji!" Her point was that since I was "Gangaji" I shouldn't be acting like someone who just got hit by a car.

Do you still meditate on any kind of a regular basis?

I don't *do* meditation, per se. Often the mind drops into a meditative state.

I can imagine someone saying, "If the result of the spiritual search is to call it off, why even start it?" How would you answer?

Well, it's not a "why" question. It's simply seeing, "Is there a spiritual search?"

From the time we're born we're all searching for something. The search begins as, "I want. How do I get?" Much later, at a certain point, some people become interested in the underlying cause of their dissatisfaction, in the mechanics of their suffering. At that point they begin to look deeper: "What is this search?"

From there they usually begin to look for how they can get enlightened or how they can escape their suffering, instead of asking the crucial question, "Who is searching?" So it's as important to start the search as to stop it. It's the discovery of the unreality of the searcher that is the end of it.

Would you say that the reason you were ready to hear Papaji when you met him was that you had already learned so much about yourself?

I don't know, but it could be. I believe that there has to be some kind of a ripening or readiness, though not necessarily in the way that it happened for me. Everybody has opportunities in their particular life to recognize that they're being tossed back and forth. Then, in that, there is a discrimination, a kind of discriminating wisdom that arises, so that they are able to hear when the truth is spoken.

Investigating how one suffers is what I talk to people about because it's what I know, but I don't think there's anything that is always necessary. It's a way I know that at least can assist people in finding clarity and a deeper understanding.

There was a certain point with Papaji where I had to realize I didn't know anything, that all of my learning was worthless. That was a very important point. I had to say, "So what if I can describe my character fixation? So what?"

Remember, I was raised a female in the South. My brother was programmed to be a doctor, but I was never programmed to be a doctor. My father wanted me to go to business school to learn to be a secretary. I had to fight to go into the liberal arts program. So for me, coming from the place I came from originally, there was an insecurity and a feeling of worthlessness. I wasn't coming from a humble mind, but a humiliated mind. Then, as I gained self-knowledge, I moved into a very strong mind that understood a lot.

Maybe the learning was necessary so that when Papaji came along, my mind could be humbled. While a strong mind may be delightful and fun, it is worthless in the face of the true investigation of who one really is. I guarantee it.

One of the ways you talk about your search is that it was for someone or something reliable to love outside yourself. Was the importance of meeting Papaji that you finally found the love object you were looking for; or was it that when you met him he convinced you to stop looking outside yourself for fulfillment?

Both! Paradoxically, mysteriously, and truly.

Your resolve to attend to what was realized with Papaji seems even more unusual than your enlightenment experiences themselves. Is resolve a matter of choice?

My experience is it's a matter of choice. When temptations arise one has the choice to fold or remain in resolve.

When I say resolve, what I mean is total, absolute surrender. Twenty-four hour, effortless resolve to be willing to see if the slightest latent tendency arises.

Since we *have* been conditioned, we have endless opportunity to see that conditioning, and to surrender it. All our latent tendencies and habits of mind are vehicles and gifts for deeper resolve, deeper surrender, deeper humbling, deeper being swept off our feet.

How important is it to have a guru or a teacher?

A guru is not necessary for everyone. There is no formula that says you need one. What I mean by a guru is the mysterious appearance, in human form, of the divine perfection of the awakened presence within. I often use the words "guru" and "teacher" interchangeably because I know "guru" is an unpopular word in the States.

Many people awaken without teachers. And there are those who find teachers who have long since departed, awake in their hearts. When you are true to Truth, if a teacher is necessary, one will appear.

For the misidentification to be finished, it was absolutely necessary for me to have a living guru. In my case I was certain I didn't need one, until it became quite clear I did. It can be just the reverse. Ramana awakened without a guru. I have met some contemporary teachers who awakened without a guru.

The great thing about having a guru, besides the unfathomable blessing of the whole phenomenon of it, is that there is an inbuilt humbling device. If you are truly surrendered to your teacher, then however your mind may get inflated, it is constantly being humbled.

LETTER TO PAPAJI, MARCH 3, 1994

Dearest Master,

    The force of your being penetrates this Ganga. In your phys-ical presence I am mute. It is only afterwards that I can perceive the depth of our meeting.

    *You are life itself. You meet me (or refuse to meet me!) in all forms, in all ways, with all faces; with smiles or frowns, at all times **UNDENIABLY YOU!** When you smile, I am drowned in joy; when you frown, I am called to vigilance. **Finally,** both smile and frown reveal this unspeakable, indefinable **TRUTH OF BEING.***

    I fall to your feet. You kill me, and I celebrate this killing as the true victory it is. Jai! Sat Guru! Jai!

    Beloved Papaji, please accept my eternal gratitude even though it is paltry in the face of THIS THAT YOU SO MERCI-FULLY AND RELENTLESSLY GIVE.

I am

Your Ganga

The mind is always waiting to capture awakening and claim ownership. I see teachers who have had strong awakening experiences, but because there is no teacher they surrender to, it turns into megalomania. People can go crazy with the energy of awakening, and with the mind coming in and co-opting that. Or, at the other end of the spectrum, they follow the mind and trivialize the awakening, which is what usually happens.

You said you didn't think the circumstances surrounding meeting Papaji were important.

I can't say for sure they weren't, but I do know there were people who woke up with him when there were hundreds of people around him. It is really not the circumstances. It is the willingness and readiness of the student.

Actually, I didn't spend that much physical time with Papaji. On the first visit I saw him every morning in satsang and then in the afternoon for tea and walks. After that visit he was surrounded by people all the time. I think I saw him privately four or five times. People will often say, "Oh, well, if I had met Papaji earlier," or, "If I could be in a smaller group with Gangaji," rather than seeing what is being offered right here, right now.

I was very lucky that I recognized Papaji's importance, and I drank him in, but I've also seen that happen with a number of people who never even spoke to him. People have had profound experiences after reading *Wake Up and Roar*, or *The Truth Is*, or *Meeting Papaji*. The teacher has to be speaking from a direct experience, but if that is coming through a book, a video, a person, or coming through in a minute or over years, what is finally relevant is the student's openness.

It's the same with the quality of the teacher. That isn't what is important. Even if the teacher is a false teacher who is not true to the awakening, people can benefit. I know people who benefit from false teachers as well as good teachers. That's because ultimately it is the student, it's not the teacher. It's really the intention of the student that is the whole show.

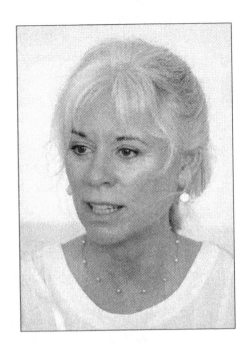

Do you consider yourself to be a guru?

No, I don't. But I truly don't consider myself to be an anything. Some time ago a lady was interviewing me and asked me about what she called the "guru" issue, or rather the "anti-guru" issue. She was very happy because she had seen "River of Freedom" and in it I say that I am not a guru. I say it several times. "I am not a guru." I could see that made her comfortable with me. She was noticeably surprised when I said, "Yes, but I am also not a human being." I said, "I'm not a woman, and yet I have experiences of being a human being and experiences of being a woman. But who I am is so much deeper." Our conversation got more interesting after that.

❖ ❖ ❖ ❖ ❖

It's clear you experience heartbreak. I remember once at a small satsang someone was telling you her heart was broken about something, as if that wasn't supposed to happen, and you said, "Why not? My heart breaks all the time." You told her your heart breaks when you read the newspaper, when someone misses a chance to awaken, when you see what your grandchildren eat. I thought that was a funny thing to say, but also very illuminating. I wonder, does your heart ever close? Do you ever experience a sense of contraction?

I have a sense in my body of certain things happening, and in that a need to withdraw, to sort of close myself off. But I wouldn't call that a heart closing. I've just read a book, *In My Hands*. It's an inspiring story about a young Polish woman who was a holocaust rescuer during World War II, so that brings Hitler to mind. I wouldn't say my heart is open to Hitler. I don't know anybody like that in my life so I'm not sure how relevant it is, but when I think of him, anger comes up at the ignorance and conditioning that gave rise to him.

When there's a real anger at something, the experience of the heart being open is not present. There is no experience of an open heart when there's an experience of anger, but actually it's impossible for the heart to close. It's only the mind that opens and closes.

If you want to know if there's a personality here, the answer is yes. There's a human being here. There's a body here. The personality and the body have their time, however long that is, and yes, they're operating here.

I think in the past there's been an idea that certain people, like the Buddha or Jesus, didn't have human qualities. I don't know if that's true. That gets taught, and I can't say it isn't so. In my experience there was an event, a something—let's not even call it "an event"—where there was a shift. But that doesn't mean that the personality, with all its tendencies, doesn't play itself out.

David Godman put out a book of conversations with people who were with Ramana and it shows you how human Ramana was, really human, in terms of anger and crankiness and all of that. That's not what usually gets said about Ramana because he's already being mythologized. The party line is that nothing played itself out in his personality, but when you read these accounts you see that actually there was a human being operating, as well as his divine radiance and sublime grace and presence.

It is essential for people to know this because everyone knows, in their own experience, there is still a personality that is acting out. What happens is, that is used as a comparison to some idealized god-figure. Then that becomes another form of, "Oh, I don't have it, I won't ever get it, I'm not worth it." That's the wheel that keeps going.

It's a delicate matter because the shift—the allowing of individual attention to fall back into the source of all attention—is huge, and so are its reverberations. It's the shift of your allegiance from the activities of your mind to the eternal presence of your Being.

Then, whether or not the personality appears again is secondary. I don't like to see it become a religion that the personality never appears again, or the humanness never appears again. What is primary is the realization of what is already free, what is still here, regardless of appearance and disappearance.

Can you talk about what it's like for you when you see a latent tendency come up? Is it a big deal or a little deal or no deal?

Well, it is an obvious deal. It is obvious. Then there is a point of choice.

So there is no struggle?

No, that doesn't sound quite right, because as the fixation arises, that is already struggle. Fixation *is* struggle. It's a particular story that goes with struggle. Since there is arising, I can't say there is no struggle. I can say there is no struggle about what the choice is.

What happens is there is an impulse that arises, but there is no impulse to continue suffering. Fixation can be stimulated by a movie, something going on in my body, or something happening in my relationships or satsang, but it just doesn't have any place to go. It doesn't have any fuel.

The truth is it could be arising and I am unaware of it. Until seen, a fixation is subconscious. So next year you'll have to ask me if it was arising. Then I will see what happened. Maybe there has been some kind of fixated behavior I have been totally unaware of all along. Maybe the whole teaching thing is fixated behavior. Who can say? Some people say that if you really wake up, you don't teach.

You said something to us in satsang that tickled me. You said, "Maybe you *are my latent tendencies."*

Yes. It may be. Then the question is what is the problem with latent tendencies, with fixation? It is not even that fixation is the problem. It is the belief that fixation is real or that fixation is the problem. *That* is the problem.

Here's a place where fixation has come up with teaching. As I said, I hardly ever know what I am going to say when I arrive at a meeting. Sometimes there will be an inspiration in getting ready, or things will come to me while I'm driving, but often I don't know. There can come an "Oh my God! What am I going to do? What am I going to say?", a residue of "You can't do it. You are not up to this."

But those thoughts have nothing to do with what I have experienced, with the absolute mystery of it. So that is definitely fixation—the belief arising that *I* am the one doing it. As soon as it gets to the thought form it is so obvious that it's a joke. Until it gets to that point it is perceived as some kind of discomfort or apprehension. Once the thought "I can't do it" arises, there is a "Hah!", and it can't continue.

So, really, there is no problem with fixation.

Has the jealousy you've spoken about come up in relation to other teachers?

I wouldn't say I feel jealous of any other teacher. There might be feelings of envy, but not jealousy, at least not the way I use the word. The way I remember jealousy, it is a much more sickening, complex emotion. Certainly I feel envious that there are certain teachers who can just teach five or seven days a week, all day. That sounds incredible. If my body could do that, then I could do what the command is to do, what the desire is to do. So, what I feel is more like, "Oh shoot, I wish I weren't so sensitive and I had that ability."

Can you say more about your sensitivity?

Oh. It knocks me out, knocks my body out. I don't know when it's going to happen. I've really looked at this, and I can't say I've come up with any answers. Since it's not true for everybody, I think it's a defect. That's the way I see it. It's a kind of defect in the nervous system, either because of the abuses on the nervous system, or just something that this nervous system was born with where energy is absorbed and not released. I'm not necessarily referring to negative energy. It's just energy, *per se*.

There was a time right after being with Papaji when I was in a state of ecstasy for weeks and it was very hard on my body. It was really wracking my body. Chinese medicine has a diagnosis, a syndrome, called excessive joy. I was experiencing that. I couldn't have imagined there would ever be a problem with joy, but it was a problem for the body. There was probably just too much energy running through the nervous system. That's why yogis develop their nervous systems, so they can handle a lot of shakti. But this nervous system was extremely sensitive as a child, and it still is. That's just the way it is.

So it's not that you take on other people's karma, which is one of the things we hear about gurus.

I've heard the stories about gurus taking on the karma of the people around them, and maybe that's so. I really don't know. It's not happening consciously with me. It's not like I'm taking on other people's stuff.

What I see is that nothing about us is static. Besides *being* the same Self, our bodies and our karma and everything is flowing in and out of each other. It seems to me that's fine if it's a healthy, balanced, centered nervous system. Then that works just fine. But if the system is not particularly healthy or is unbalanced, it doesn't work so well. This is my theory. I don't know if it's correct, but my nervous system is not a good, solid, strong one.

That's why you need to rest.

Yes. I have to rest a lot. And beauty is really important, just to see beauty. To me it is absolutely beautiful here, looking out into the canyon. Just look at these trees, these oak trees. I can feel their energy coming into my system, and there's a letting go. It was good in Stinson Beach, where I used to live, because of the ocean. Whether just seeing the ocean translates something into my unconscious so there is a release and a cleansing, or whether it's the actual ocean air, there is an experience of the ocean taking it all away, taking it all. It's very nice to swim too. That also helps.

If I'm in a retreat for a week I may be surrounded by beauty, and the experiences in the retreat are certainly beautiful, but the nervous system is taking blows. That's not always true. I don't know if it's going to be true until after the retreat is over.

When I was a massage therapist and an acupuncturist there were all kinds of visualizations I knew for protection, but it still happened. So, I don't really have any tricks. I just have to rest and allow myself to recharge. It's what happens with this body. Maybe it'll stop sometime.

Another thing we hear about people who awaken is that there are signs in their childhood of what will happen. When I began interviewing you I was convinced that what happened to you when you were six and you experienced your body disappearing was one of those signs.

Someone was interviewing me just the other day and he said he'd seen it in so many enlightened people, that when they were six something extraordinary happened that was a sign of things to come. To this man, that experience of the body disappearing was a foreshadowing of enlightenment. But, as I said, it's just as easy to see that experience as a little six-year-old girl having an anxiety attack.

Occasionally I get a letter from someone who knew me before, and when they discover me on the internet or come to a satsang, they say, "You know, I always saw something very special in you." The past is so colored by the present though, that it's hard to know whether to believe them. I don't know that the people who say there was something striking about me would be saying it if I hadn't met Papaji and this awakening hadn't happened. There are plenty of people who would say the opposite. It's a funny thing the way the mind arranges it all.

It seems like you stopped really caring about your negative thoughts before your awakening. Is that right?

Well, I think it was before the waking up. It was really in discovering the enneagram of character fixation and realizing that the negative thoughts were only habits. I would say in awakening there was the recognition that even though thoughts are powerful and can cause harm, internally and externally, they don't make me impure. They don't touch the purity. So there is not exactly a welcoming, but an understanding.

If a small child has a tantrum you are not threatened that the child is going to actually blow up the house.

There are childish habits that arise in us all, but they just don't mean anything. I think that is part of the grace of this lineage: the recognition that it is the Silence that is the true face of oneself.

Are you sure "this Gangaji person's" happiness doesn't depend on circumstances, like having a good relationship, or a great job, or a relatively easy life style?

I would say no, I'm not sure of that. It's the opposite. I can be unhappy just because it is raining. That's an outer circumstance. If I am having a pain somewhere in my body, I am not happy.

When I said "happiness" I meant the overarching happiness that includes all states.

Let's not call it "happiness" then. Let's ask, "Does Gangaji's freedom, or does Gangaji's fulfillment, have anything to do with circumstances?"

Okay. Does it?

No. It's unconditional. Until I met Papaji what I was looking for was to always be happy, to never be depressed, sad or angry. But looking for happiness kept me bound to preferred states of mind. When you're searching for "always happy" your reference for who you are is your emotions, and you overlook the ground of fulfillment that is even closer than your emotions, and always here.

❖ ❖ ❖ ❖ ❖

I've heard you talk about humans in a way that gave me a valuable perspective. I want to repeat what you said because so many of us are looking for a way to view what's going on in the world today.

You said, "As a species, as primates, we are very aggressive. That is part of our animal nature. Aggression is power, and power is pleasure. We have loved power over everything. Individually to different degrees, and definitely collectively, to a very dangerous degree. And so we have denied our connection. We have overlooked the innocence, the open heart, in favor of the closed fist, over and over, many times in a day. And we are seeing the results of that all over the world."

Do the current circumstances in the world affect you?

Oh yes.

Is there anything you can say that might be helpful?

Only to be true to yourself. Be true to yourself. Some people have an idea that waking up means that you aren't concerned with feeling what's happening in the world, but in my experience I am more concerned. What's happening in the Middle East right now is so sad. It is so sad, I cry. I don't say that that's a requirement for waking up, but that is just the way it shows up here.

People sometimes ask me how politically active they should be, but I don't tell people what they "should" do. What I know, and what I tell them, is that when you trust the stillness, when you trust the spaciousness, instead of trusting the mind, what *to* do is revealed in what you *do* do.

Ever since I began speaking I have encouraged people to take advantage of their great luck in having relative freedom. Most people on the planet don't have this—the time to think, the freedom to speak, the possibility to be still. We should know our circumstances could change very quickly but for this brief time that we have relative freedom, how will our luck be used? To be worried about whether we will lose it, or to take this time of opportunity to discover the depths?

(The following conversation took place on October 6th, 2001, three and a half weeks after 9-11, and one day before the bombing began in Afghanistan.)

I'm glad you came to interview me, and I'm very happy to talk to you today, but I don't want to talk about my personal story. I can't put my attention into that when there's such a huge world story unfolding.

Yes. On my way here I wondered if you might rather talk about what's happening in the world and what has come up around it.

It's the only thing we can speak about right now. It's not even possible for me to talk about my past. What difference does it make? What's happening now to all of us is what must be attended to.

I know you went to New York a few days after the September 11th attack to meet Eli, and that you witnessed the rubble that was left of the World Trade Center. Do you think actually being there made it more real for you?

I don't know. Just seeing the images on television was very, very strong. I've heard people say that the attack on the World Trade Center is not a big deal, that we Americans are only dealing with what countless nations have been dealing with through the ages, in one form or another. But I don't subscribe to that. Even though there's nothing new about horror, the moment of horror is always new. This is a new moment in our history. We have to attend to it with great honesty. The comparison that I get to, between ourselves and other nations, is that it's like

having a friend whose child has died. I feel so much compassion for my friend and I grieve so deeply for her, but it's not the same as if I lose my own child. It can't be.

I'm speaking as an American right now. Seeing fellow Americans die by the thousands, being incinerated, jumping out of the windows of their office buildings because it's better than the alternative, seeing it happen here in our country, not in some foreign place, has to have a profound impact on us. So for me there's a sorrow that comes up, a real grieving, and that grieving has a course of its own.

We have lived such sheltered, insulated lives, with a strong belief in our own invulnerability. Now that belief has been shattered. Now it is obvious that what will happen is unknowable, completely unknowable, and this is a profound change.

I remember the first time I heard you say, "I don't know whether we'll make it as a species on the planet," and how deeply that went in. I appreciated the reminder of the obvious, that there are no guarantees.

That's right. There are no guarantees. It's very important that each one of us meets whatever comes up now. It's part of the tempering, the maturing, that is thrust upon us. Grieving takes time. When a mother loses her child, the next day you don't say, "Okay, that's finished, now get over it." It's a mistake to rush back into activity, not to take the time that's required to experience what is evoked by this blow, whether it's anger, sorrow, despair, or some kind of numbness—then experience what is under that.

❖ ❖ ❖ ❖ ❖

Gangaji, do you like giving satsang?

I love it! I have loved giving satsang from the first meeting. I look forward to each meeting. It is a challenge, but I love the challenge. The uncontrollability of the meetings is exciting, and I don't mind being on the edge. I am always happy to direct attention away from suffering, and toward finding the truth of who it is that suffers.

What is required on my end is seeing what is fresh, what is alive in each moment. It is not always comfortable or pleasant or fun, but it is always wonderful and mysterious. The sharing of the realization is equal to the

A PUBLIC MEETING IN THE MID-NINETIES

discovery of it, and is finally the same. Being in satsang deepens the discovery.

LETTER TO PAPAJI, AUGUST 11, 1990

My Father,

The joy of satsang is almost unbearable. There is no one to speak this unspeakable Truth with - your presence animates all. We sing praises only to YOU WHO ARE OUR VERY SELF.

The profoundness and simplicity of your presence humbles me in this highest honor of offering myself over and over as your food.

I KNOW NOTHING BUT YOUR LOVE.

Your servant,

Gangaji

Have your satsangs changed over the years? Have you gotten better at it?

In terms of how it's changed over the years, I can't say. I don't know whether my skills have improved. I know that the thrust of where it's coming from is exactly the same.

It does seem to me as though people are listening to me more. There was a phase in the early years of my being tested and watched, and retested and watched. Now people have tested me and watched me to whatever degree was necessary for them, and they're listening more. I see less confrontation.

Having these meetings is always an honor. It is an honor that people will come to hear this teaching, that they trust this form with their attention for an hour and a half or two. I never, ever, have lost the sense of the honor it is, the honor that Papaji gave me. What a joy! And you honor me by wanting to talk to me, and the same with the people who read this. So I thank you.

Can you tell who will be attracted to you or this teaching?

No. It's really a surprise all around.

Don't you see a pattern?

What I see in the people who are attracted to this teaching is a kind of intelligence. Intelligence and maturity. By intelligence I don't mean a strong intellect. That can be there or not. And maturity doesn't necessarily mean long spiritual practice, nor is it related to any age. But those two qualities seem to be necessary, because nothing is offered by this teaching.

Is there anything that you receive from your students?

Oh yes. So much. Myself! I receive myself over and over. They give me love, so it's a beautiful, exquisite, intimate relationship. And they break my heart, so it's also a challenge in discovering, even deeper, always, the fulfillment in one's self.

WITH BHAVO, A DEAR STUDENT, BEFORE HIS DEATH

What do you want this rendering of your life to transmit?

The presence of Truth, the presence right now of Truth. And the invitation to surrender to that, right now.

This experience with you clarifies the invitation. I hope no one gets caught up in your story. You so obviously aren't.

Well, that is what I want. For the book to encourage awakening, not distract from it. I like the working title, *"Just Like You."* It is a tricky business though. As with all expressions, it can be used either to demean or to wake up. So that will be the edge: to recognize that in the ordinariness of you and me, there is the sublime presence of Truth.

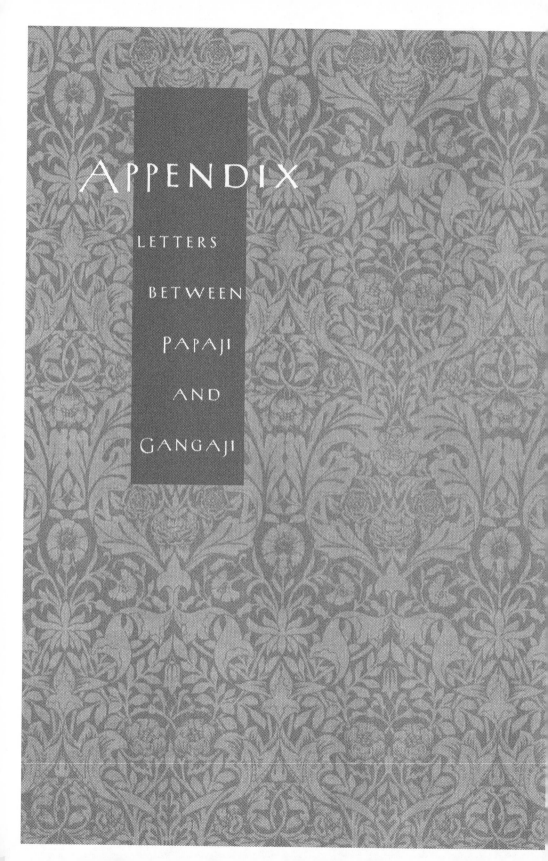

APPENDIX

LETTERS

BETWEEN

PAPAJI

AND

GANGAJI

THESE LETTERS WERE *selected from those Gangaji and Papaji exchanged between 1990 and 1997.*

July 29, 1990

Dearest Self as Poonjaji, Master,

How I love to talk with you - in silence and with words. My only bliss is the devourment by your majesty - and that is offered by you everywhere in everything. I am both serene and ecstatic - I embrace the world with fervor, as I see in it only Self, and with detachment, as I know it to be form. How is it possible? Only through your incomprehensible love, which by your grace feeds on this form as Gangaji. This body quakes in the wonder ever unfolding, fathomless in depth, forever unknowable.

The "I" that seemingly was and who judged and evaluated is reduced to ashes as the I THAT IS AND ALWAYS WAS and is no I, but ONE WITH NO OTHER.

Is there no end? Has it always been so? My mind reels in wonder and surrender. It is consumed by the very Self that gave life and then resurrects it to serve as Perfect Servant to Perfect Master.

There is less and less holding back - courage and conviction fill the space left vacant - fear and doubt instantly disappear. Use me as you will - I am only yours.

Self as Ganga, Servant

November 6, 1990

Dearest Papaji,

Jaxon* and I are visiting one of the most beautiful places on earth - Yosemite National Park. We have just left the San Francisco area, where we visited many people you know. Satsang was, as always, totally surprising and wonderful.

Dearest Master, how is it possible for one of your students who has realized that which is beyond enlightenment to begin to follow the mind? I must understand how it is possible for this to happen.

Your daughter, your own Self, your eternal servant,
Ganga

*Eli Jaxon Bear

November 7, 1990

Dearest Father,

*I kiss your magnificent feet, Dearest One, in deepest grati-
tude for your introduction to my Holy of Holies Grandfather,
Ramana Maharshi.*

*Tonight he answered the question I wrote to you yesterday.
In his indescribably radiant silence, he clearly reminded me that
ALL THIS HAS NOTHING TO DO WITH ME. ANY
INTERFERENCE AS DOER WITH ANYTHING IS
UNNECESSARY!*

*Dearest Father, this totally unexpected, UNIMAGINABLE
Darshan given by Bhagavan Ramana is beyond the beyond. Life
immortal in form and formlessness! IMPOSSIBLE TRUTH!*

*The deep quiet bliss I feel when I look into my grandfather's
eyes is beyond my tongue to speak - no words can ever form
around or even point to this experience. To say that is possible is
the meaning of blasphemy. Unspeakable, unthinkable mute Bliss!*

> *All love,*
> *Ganga, daughter of Sri Poonjaji, Maharishi*
> *granddaughter of Bhagavan Ramana*

November 22, 1990

My very dear Daughter,

    I am proud to be a father of such a daughter, who stated that "no good or bad news" would or could ever touch her, who has gone beyond the yonder shore, not to return or abide anywhere, being SELF undefinable "I AM."

    My father, your grandfather, is all along with you wherever you are. Have no doubt about it. What you say, that was what I had to reply to you and dear Jaxon, but quickly I received your letter dated 11-7-90, and thus I am very pleased to read my own words from your mouth. All this or all that has nothing to do with a non-doer.

    My Master has given you Darshan as He did to me. You are blessed, you have crossed this ocean of samsara. What a luck.

    When you left Lucknow I told you to speak about what so far remained unspoken, unthinkable, unimaginable, and unknown. This you very well pointed out, in mute gesture.

    Speak more to me! I like to hear more and more. I will never be tired of listening to this romance, where do I melt.

    You have well deserved the name "GangaJee," dropped on you by the Ma Ganga, who liberates the beings by a mere touch, thought, or sight. The Consciousness resting in the hearts of all beings.

    This letter will always remain to continue writing.

        Your Papa,
        Poonjaji

February 4, 1991

Dearest Beloved Master,

*I am **continually** wonderstruck at the profound*
*   **simplicity** of the Truth of oneSelf,*
Ever abiding, yet completely ungraspable in time or place.
The bliss of continual surrender, which is more subtle even than
*   bliss,*
Permeating everything: all forms, all directions, all actions
Bursting this heart, while causing not even a ripple.
What can be said? Always simply nothing!

Your
Ganga

March 4, 1991

Very Dear Gangaji,

I read your wonderful letter.
*My dear daughter, **speak more**.*
*I like you speak to me. As you speak, so do I hear you from my own **SELF**.*
This wonder.
I am in love with my own Self.

Your Papa,
Poonjaji

May 16, 1991

Ma Ganga Ji,

So many people from USA & Europe tell me that they have been helped by Ganga Ji. I am so happy my Ganga, during my lifetime, is working to remove the ignorance from the minds of people. You have to dedicate your entire life for the good of all beings of this planet.

Ramana means "one who is all pervading and dwells in the Heart of all Beings."

With much love,
HWL Poonja

July 2, 1991

Dearest Father,

In my deep bliss and gratefulness, I often forget the immense nightmare most people are suffering with. My unspeakable luck in meeting you, MY SOURCE, drops me to the ground - to the dust of your Holy Feet. If I can share this luck, I can in some way repay what can never be paid. "My" life is over. This life form lives solely for sharing the Truth of return to what was never, IN TRUTH, lost.

May all beings be happy.

In true love and devotion,
Ganga

July 24, 1991

Dearest Beloved Master,

    We are beginning our time in Europe here in Amsterdam. Tomorrow we fly to Vienna.

    You enclosed a letter from a kind man, a long-time disciple of yours from Madras (I could not read his name). Please thank him for me and let him know that those who speak of "Toni wandering through California" dig in graveyards and run from ghosts. This "Toni" blessedly drowned in the Ganga at her Master's feet. There is only Ganga left, and she simply flows into and merges with her Source - The Ocean Poonjaji - each moment. What gets flooded through this relentless embrace of Self, who can say?

                                Your
                                Ganga

October 17, 1991

Dearest Father,

Who could ever hope to describe the joy of your lover. Even the sight of your handwriting is enough. How lucky we, your children, are. Whatever tales of woe are dreamed, they are less than dust in the LIGHT OF THE TRUTH OF YOU.

Dearest One, I live, breathe, eat, sleep, drink, and die in YOU. You have taken "me" completely. What is left is ONLY YOU. Blessed, Holy TRUTH OF YOU.

There are many people who come here six days a week for Satsang. I only see YOUR FACE. They ask questions - I only hear You speak. They laugh - It is Your laugh. They recognize oneself as they see You. Once having seen You, there is ONLY YOU.

My beloved Self, in form I am
your obedient daughter,
Ganga

July 26, 1992

Dearest Beloved Heart of Hearts,

*Once the mind is still, the MIND of the mind makes ITSELF known. In this KNOWING, the Ganga blissfully merges into YOU - never to be seen again except at your bidding. As you bid, I assume name and form - As you bid, I am. What need have I of **anything - any power** or **any experience?** As I AM DEVOTION TO YOU, I am complete. Form is nothing in the force of This Love - Formless is nothing in the force of This Love. This Love THAT YOU ARE IS THE MASTER OF ALL REALMS.*

In Your blessed service,
Ganga

December 25, 1994

Dear Gangaji,

This morning I read the transcript of your interview by Richard to the members of Satsang Bhavan. It is excellent. Every one loved it. We will arrange to send you the tape of Tuesday along with music and songs by Americans, Italians, and Germans.

I send you my good wishes and blessing to live for long time to awaken people. A group of 15 people is here from Sedona, AZ who brought this tape.

With much love —Papa

May 11, 1995

Dearest Divine Master,

By your glance, your touch, and your word you have caused the desert to bloom!

A life wasted on personal suffering is revealed to exist only in thought.

In raining your divine grace on that life, awe and gratitude bloom. What you have done cannot be spoken. The life that remains in your wake is the proof.

This life belongs to **YOU WHO IS THAT ONE**.

Your

Ganga

June 22, 1997

Dearest Papaji,

The longer this form continues, the more the depth and clarity of your wisdom reveals itself.

I am prostrate before you - who reveals the unspeakable reconciliation of all.

I love you, Papaji. The jewel you reveal to me is offered to all I meet - by your grace alone -

You are the jewel! You are immeasurable.

Your daughter in love,
Ganga

From the Publishers

We cannot thank Gangaji enough for her time, her attention, and her unwavering kindness—while we worked on the manuscript, and always. As she says, her life didn't *really* begin until she met Papaji. Even so, she allowed this biography of her life-in-progress to be published. Her generosity in sharing herself pierces our hearts.

We want to thank Gwyn Hall for donating her valuable help as transcriber and researcher. Her enthusiasm and constancy were vital to the creation of *Just Like You*.

Many thanks to Dan Baumbach for the gift of his cover photographs, and the series of pictures of Gangaji in the conversation section. Working with him was a delight. And to Sally Ruane for devotedly keeping Papaji's and Gangaji's correspondence, and helping with the selection and presentation of the letters. Her input during the unfoldment of the book was always appreciated.

We are ever grateful to the Gangaji Foundation, and to the Bay Area volunteers, for all they do to get Gangaji's message into the world, as well as for their many favors.

We gladly acknowledge Lynne Abels, Mitch Clogg,

Eleanor Cooney, Olin Garfield, and Susan McNeil for their help with editing, and thank each one for their gracious support. Also, Theresa Whitehill. The design of *Just Like You* reflects her lovely clarity.

And, dear reader, we wholeheartedly thank you for your interest in Gangaji and what she points to. It is a blessing to be able to share this book.

Roslyn and Bruce Moore

CONTACTS

Books, videos, and audio recordings by and about Ramana Maharshi, Papaji and Gangaji are available from the Gangaji Foundation. You can go to www.gangaji.org for ordering information, as well as for Gangaji's schedule and a wide variety of other offerings.

The Gangaji Foundation   {ph} 800-267-9205
2245 Ashland Street   {fax} 541-552-9921
Ashland, OR 97520   info@gangaji.org

Just Like You and *Meeting Papaji* can also be ordered directly from Roslyn Moore. Inquiries are welcome.

{ph} 707-964-2630
{fax} 707-964-7353
brmoore@mcn.org

CPSIA information can be obtained
at www.ICGtesting.com
Printed in the USA
FSHW020422190620
71201FS